Whigmaleeries: A

Cover Illustration: **Dee Varley**

TABLE OF CONTENTS

Introduction – Wheeler's Irregulars

Author Summaries ... 1

Div Ye Min? ... 2

Dennis the Menace in the 21st Century	Edwin Webster	4
War Story – Daddy's Girl?	Clarissa Kelly	5
The Clydeside Blitz	George Crossan	6
The Locarno	Adelaide Gordon	10
A Strange Picture	Beatrice Davidson	11
A Visit to the Maritime Museum	Clarissa Kelly	13
The Wedding Dress	George Crossan	15
The Common Caul'	Edwin Webster	16
Rock and Roll	Clarissa Kelly	17
A Coat Hanger	George Crossan	19
The Worst Night of the Blitz April 1943	Adelaide Gordon	21
The Fabulous Fifties	Beatrice Davidson	22
Slum Clearance	Clarissa Kelly	24
Safety Razor	George Crossan	26

Once Upon a Time...

Local Enterprise	Edwin Webster	28
The Dark at the Bottom of the Stairs	Adelaide Gordon	31
Hunter's Moon	Edwin Webster	33
Eckie's Ghost	Anne Flann	35
Show A Leg!	Edwin Webster	37
The Purple Hat [1]	Clarissa Kelly	39
The Purple Hat [2]	Clarissa Kelly	41
Council Tax Made Simple	Edwin Webster	43
The Performance	Anne Flann	44
A Gey Aul' Desert Sang	Edwin Webster	47
The Train Journey	Sylvia Chesser	49
Twa Half-Croons	Edwin Webster	51

A Bourach...

The Cages	Anne Flann	53
Be it Ever So Humble	Edwin Webster	55
The Waitress	Anne Flann	56
Greetings	Edwin Webster	58
A New Leaf	Sylvia Chesser	60
Travelling Companions	Anne Flann	62
Media Star	Edwin Webster	64
Family Album	Anne Flann	65
Ooyah! Ooyah! Ooyah!	Edwin Webster	66
The Stamp of Adventure	Sylvia Chesser	68

Top Marks

An Affa Sair Belly	Edwin Webster	71
The Lone Seat	Anne Flann	72
Millicent	Clarissa Kelly	74
A Red Letter Day	George Crossan	76
Right or Wrong?	Edwin Webster	79
Teacher	Anne Flann	80
Angus	George Crossan	82
R.I.P.	Edwin Webster	84

For the Bairns...

The Whistle	Adelaide Gordon	86
Bubba – The Lion Cub	Anne Flann	88
Crathes Castle's Visitor	Sylvia Chesser	91
The Magic Button	Clarissa Kelly	93
The Charioteer	Anne Flann	95
A Kitten Named George	Adelaide Gordon	97
The Three-Legged Race	Sylvia Chesser	98
A Child's Fairy Tale	George Crossan	100

Epilogue

Finality	George Crossan	100

*Whigmaleerie (-y; -ies) n. (scot.): an ornamental bauble, an indefinable trinket, a fanciful notion, an artful caprice, a charming contrivance.

Introduction – Wheeler's Irregulars
Ed Webster

I coined the title of this piece to describe the group of writers I belong to. We meet on a regular basis but in an irregular manner, if you grasp my meaning. Fifteen persons agreed to attend the first meeting, but only twelve turned up on the day. This shrank to a core of four or five, plus one or two others showing up now and again. Later, the remains of our group united with the tail end of a second group and the result is the present body of scribblers which gathers in the Art Gallery of a Wednesday morning. We are all 'of a certain age' and each one of us has a personal definition of that phrase.

Our mentor, Les Wheeler, is a fan of Bernard Cornwell, creator of the Sharpe novels, which are set during the Napoleonic wars. Military units of the period sometimes bore the name of their commanding officer e.g. Sharpe's Skirmishers, Raleigh's Rifles, Hunter's Light Horse etc.

Thus Wheeler's Irregulars reflects our organiser and advisor and one facet of his literary interest. It also reflects the nature of our own group of writers, regular in attendance but sometimes irregular in production of finished items for our proposed goal – a book, or books for school-children and for members of the general public.

Over the period of time we have worked and skived together, I have developed a certain regard for the group and for its members; this is a personal tribute to them. When our meetings finally come to an end, there will be a gap in my life.

Author Summaries

Adelaide Gordon

I started writing stories when I joined a group at Provost Skene's House. First we wrote about the artefacts on display and slowly started getting other stories together. Lisa was introduced to our group and with her advice and encouragement we started to scribble and scribble. It was amazing! She put our stories together and worked hard to get our book published.

Clarissa Kelly

Clarissa Kelly was born in Aberdeen in 1940, where she has lived all her life. She is married with two grown-up sons and five grandchildren. Her avid interest in reading led her to join the writers' group when she retired. Her other hobbies include golf, yoga and tap-dancing.

Sylvia Chesser

Aberdeen
A creative writer ......um......
Slovenia
She is writing this while waiting for a train in Slovenia. A loud conversation is coming from the nearby café. She wishes she could communicate and somehow lighten the atmosphere with humour. Like now, she is happy travelling but also enjoys a variety of pursuits in her native Aberdeen. She is happily married with two grown-up children.

Beatrice Davidson

Born and bred in Aberdeen. Married to a County policeman (now retired). Fifteen houses since marrying. Now living in Kingswells and hopefully grounded. Two daughter, two sons-in-law, four grandchildren.

One of Wheeler's Irregulars due mainly to too many irons in the fire.

Now engrossed in writing a family history purely for my grandchildren. Oh! Why didn't I listen more carefully to the tales my grandparents told me? How fascinating it would have been if my grandmother had written about her life and times.

George Crossan

George Crossan, formerly of Glasgow, came to Aberdeen in 1966. He retired, early, in 1980. With a background including theatre, television, teaching, lecturing, etc., he was attracted to the Writers' Group, mainly because of the opportunity it offered to write about some of the artefacts treasured and preserved in the Art Gallery and Museums of Aberdeen. When the purpose of the group changed, he was happy to continue as a member.

Edwin Webster

Coffin-dodging Aberdonian. Idler, dreamer and professional pauper. Harmless and quite docile in natural habitat, but liable to bark if patronised or poked with a stick. Has never recovered from the extinction of the dinosaur and the invention of the wheel. Hates almost everything.

anne flann

Aberdonian, retired photo/journalist with an expatriate American community newspaper. Now turned to poetry and story-writing to fill the gap after 17 years of interesting events, fascinating people – and sheer hard slog. Nothing changes!

Whigmaleeries: A Word in Your Lug

Div Ye Min?

Dennis the Menace in the 21st Century   Edwin Webster

Dennis spat into a flowerbed, kicked the head off a carnation, and lobbed a stone at the black and white cat sneaking along the top of a fence. A thump and a screech indicated that he had found the target.

"Y' know, Gnasher," he said, addressing his fearsome wire-haired Abyssinian tripehound, "I'm fed up with bein' a cartoon character. Look at me. I'm fifty years old. I'm still wearing a stupid stripy jumper an' short trousers an' I've got knobbly knees an' a daft haircut. All I ever do is cause mischief an' play tricks on people. What a life! I'm bored."

Gnasher grunted in sympathy, looked at his master with as much affection as he could muster (which still left him looking as if he was chewing broken glass), then took off at considerable speed in pursuit of the black and white cat. When he returned, spitting fur, Dennis once again addressed his faithful hound: "Right, Gnasher. I've made my mind up. I'm going to talk to the Editor and have myself updated. I'm going to be a 21st Century Dennis. C'mon."

Some time later, Dennis and Gnasher were ushered into the august presence of the Beano Editor and Dennis stated his case, emphasising his desire to be brought up to date. The Editor, a very wise and patient man, listened carefully, pondered for a few minutes, then gave his opinion,

"Look at it this way, Dennis. If our cartoonists brought you bang up to date and made you fifty years old, you'd be a dad, maybe even a grandad, and you'd be responsible for bringing up a Dennis, perhaps several little Dennises. Then you'd be the one who had all the tricks played on him. You'd spend all your time being a victim of menacing. How would you like that?"

Dennis screwed his face up, scowled ferociously, thought as hard as he could and then conceded,

"Yeah. You're right, boss. It wouldn't be any fun. One Dennis is enough for Beanotown. I'm better off as I am. C'mon, Gnash. Let's nip down the park. I'll try out my new water pistol and you can dig up some flowerbeds. Let's go!"

© Copyright Edwin Webster 2004

War Story – Daddy's Girl?   Clarissa Kelly

The little girl sat playing on the rug in front of the fire. It was the only space available in the small cramped kitchen, which also had a double bed occupying most of the room. Unlike some tenement flats there was no bed recess in this older building.

It was summer time and the room was warm and stuffy. The little girl liked it best when on cold nights the fire was lit and she could play with her toys toasting herself before the inevitable bedtime and the cold front room.

Just then the door opened, her mother looked up rather quickly from the sink. It was her grandmother visiting from her home upstairs. The little girl's round face, framed with straight white blonde hair lit up with a beaming smile when she saw her grandmother.

Her mother and grandmother talked quietly together and now and then would glance in her direction as she played. She was aware that her mother had been acting different all day but she was too young to interpret her body language. Her grandmother had been in and out during the afternoon and her visits had increased as the evening approached.

Suddenly the door opened, her mother rushed to the door followed by her grandmother. They were squealing and laughing and the little girl was amazed she had never seen big people act like this in all her five long years. What was going on? There was a tall man standing just inside the door, he was wearing a uniform and in the excitement his hat had fallen to the floor. He had a large canvas bag with him. Who was he? The little girl wondered.

By this time the excitement had subsided slightly and the little girl abandoned her toys and stood up. She was confused and took refuge behind her grandmother clutching onto her skirts and daring to peep round to see what her mother was doing. She couldn't understand what was happening. Her mother had her arms round the tall man's neck and was speaking so fast the little girl could not make out what she was saying.

The tall man in the uniform saw the little girl and came towards her. He bent down to speak to her. She clung more tightly to her grandmother. The tall man lifted her up in his arms and held her round the waist. She could smell the mustiness of his uniform and feel the roughness of the material against her skin. The tall man then tried to kiss the little girl. She could smell the stale odour of his breath and the feel of his unshaven face against her young skin was too much for her. She bent her body back away from the tall man's face as he held her firmly round the waist and against his body, she lay into his face with her tiny fists using all her strength, crying and shaking as she did so.

Through her crying and distress she heard her mother's voice. "It's your Daddy. He's come home from the war. Give him a kiss".

© Copyright Clarissa Kelly 2004

The Clydeside Blitz   George Crossan

- The word blitz is really a contraction of the German word blitzkrieg ('lightning war'): of the type in World War II that overtook Denmark, Norway, Belgium, Holland and France in the early part of 1940, and Yugoslavia and Greece in 1941. In a campaign in part to prepare the way for an invasion of Britain, Germany concentrated its superior air power on bombing raids on British airfields and towns. This became known as The Blitz.

- Although London bore most of the brunt of these raids, other cities suffered damage and casualties, some more severe than others - including Coventry, Clydeside and Aberdeen.

My story begins in the East End of Glasgow, on the evening of Thursday, 13 March, 1941.

My two pals and I used to meet, weekly, in Shettleston about 7 pm, on a Thursday, where we would board a tramcar going to Paisley. Our pleasure was to spend an evening skating at Paisley Ice Rink. The journey would last about an hour.

Unfortunately (or so we thought), one of my friends was late. Annoyingly, he arrived just as the tram was leaving its stop. We decided to run for it. Two of us managed to jump on while it was moving. The third - the cause of it all - damned his reputation a bit more by failing to get aboard. There was nothing else for it but to jump off again – a skill most of us had developed over time.

There was no serious recrimination when we rejoined one another. We were pals. We were young, in our teens, when living seemed always to be in the present continuous tense. We forgave easily.

To wait for the next tram, would mean that we would have a much shorter time at the rink. The cost of admission would be the same – an important factor in our deliberations. Additionally, because of the war, the last trams home were earlier than we would have liked. You might think, because there was a war on, that we were unduly frivolous to be thinking of enjoying ourselves. Not so. Although we lived in a world of restrictions and deprivations, there were few complaints. You adapted. After a time, life seemed fairly normal.

Having decided that skating was no longer feasible, we went to the pictures.

During the performance, we were interrupted by the manager's sudden appearance in front of the screen. The film had stopped. 'I have a special announcement to make', he said, calmly. 'The air raid sirens have gone. If some wish to leave the theatre, they should do so now, quietly. We shall continue with the film until its end.' Quite a number left. But we decided to stay. We wanted our money's worth.

Because all forms of entertainment were required to finish early, we were soon on the street again. There was an air of excitement. It was a clear, moonlight night. The sky was criss-crossed by moving searchlights. Anti-aircraft guns were firing. High above our heads, shells were exploding. In the midst of the noise was another sound; one I had not heard before. Its rhythmic droning sounded sinister and menacing; unmistakeably, the sonorous sound of heavily-laden bombers. I was familiar with the sound of fighter aircraft (I was an air cadet) but not German bombers.

Occasionally, we could see one clearly, seemingly transfixed in the glare of searchlights with puffs of exploding shells around it. They were all fairly high up, pushed aloft by the presence of a ring of barrage balloons whose hanging chains threatened their survival, if they were to come lower. One balloon burst into flames and floated, silently, like a fiery shroud, towards the ground.

We had no fear. The imagery was dramatic and alluring. Although the sound seemed to carry a threat, the planes' truly aggressive intention was muted by distance. In isolation, the pictorial imagery was magnetic and exhilarating.

By this time, air-raid-wardens were all over the place urging people to take shelter. Thoughts of our families began now to hold our attention. It was time to go home. We separated to go our different ways. There was no public transport, and I resorted to running. As I came nearer to my home, I heard a very loud noise that caused me some apprehension. I stopped an air-raid warden. Did he know what it was? With all the confidence of a person who thinks he ought to know, but didn't, he said, 'Yes'. He named a street. 'A landmine has just fallen there.' Since that street was near my home, I ran even faster.

When I reached there, there was no sign of alarm. The surrounding streets were empty, and moderately quiet. One could hear the occasional sounds of clanging service-vehicles and, of course, the recurring throbbing of the planes. Inside my home, my family were sitting in a circle, on chairs that had been brought into the lobby from every available quarter. We were a big family and found some self support in numbers.

The sound of battle lessened. Eventually, the all-clear sounded about eight o'clock in the morning.

Surprisingly – or, perhaps, not surprisingly, depending on your experience of human beings under test - most people turned up for work on Friday, as usual.

People talked a lot about possible targets, and there were strong rumours that Clydebank and its shipyards had suffered extensive damage. The official communiqué released later in the day was vague. But one piece of news on the grapevine emphasized the gravity of that night's event: the report that the tram we had meant to travel on was hit by a bomb on its way to Paisley Ice Rink.

The glamorous, pictorial imagery of the early part of the evening disappeared in the clear morning air.

At nightfall, at much the same time as the night before, the sirens rang out again. On this occasion, they seemed more plaintive. As the planes came nearer, more guns opened up. We were more aware of their menace. The curiosity of the night before had changed to uneasy expectation. Fingers of searchlights groped about the sky looking for targets. Tiring of waiting for a hit, I moved back into the house.

I don't remember how long we sat there, before the bomb fell. Its sound, as it thundered through the air, was ominous and frightening. We all slumped, tentatively, with embarrassment, towards the floor, knowing that this is what we were supposed to do, but feeling pretty daft about doing it.

It fell near us, but not near enough for its explosion to affect us directly. We waited, half sitting, half kneeling on the floor, for whatever else would follow. Nothing came. After a short interval, we struggled back onto our seats again. We tried to guess where the bomb might have exploded, and who might be the casualties - but we didn't dare go and see. Later, an air-raid warden, hurrying past, told us that a house nearby had been hit, but that there were no casualties.

Morning came. The 'all clear' sounded. Rumoured stories circulated about possible targets, likely damage and possible victims.

In fact, at our end of the city, there were few injuries and only minor damage. But more stories of the devastation caused by a second night's battering of the people of Clydebank gave rise to considerable apprehension and speculation.

(BBC News Picture Gallery)

A week later, I went down the river to Clydebank. The town had been closed for a number of days, so that the dead and wounded could be removed, the homeless evacuated and insecure buildings reinforced or knocked down. I walked most of the way, about two hours from where I lived. I was alone.

It is difficult to find words to explain my reason for going. I suppose I had watched the first two acts of a drama, and needed to see the third.

Even now, I can see the desolate streets and strangled thoroughfares choked by debris; skeletal buildings, still standing precariously, with jagged outlines making odd shapes in the skyline. Unsupported, broken staircases perched among them. Shattered windows mixed with undamaged ones. Signs of human habitation were palpable: mirrors, cupboards, family pictures - all attached to toothy outlines of bomb-battered tenements. I felt out of scale with my surroundings, able to inspect the interiors of so many houses at a glance.

The silence was oppressive. I don't remember meeting anyone there. Maybe I was too pre-occupied with the awfulness of such destruction. I was in my teens. I had never seen such wilful annihilation. I didn't dare think of the casualties. (Later, given as 1000 dead and 1100 injured – though revised downward, some time afterwards.) Although there were no bodies, their very absence was creepy and unnatural.

Coming home, I passed a solitary, low-built cottage. The windows and roof were smashed. My view was into the bedroom. A double bed had not been slept in. It was covered by a plain, white, unblemished bed-spread. A long, tilted, iron beam had pierced the roof like a lance, and penetrated its stain-free purity. Only the blood was missing.

© Copyright George Crossan 2004

The Locarno   Adelaide Gordon

It was Monday night. I was looking forward to going dancing with my friends at the Locarno Ballroom. We met at our usual place, at the statue of Queen Victoria at the end of George Street. This was a very popular place to meet in those days.

After checking our coats into the cloakroom, we changed into our high-heeled dance shoes. The best dancers packed the place on Mondays. There was a great atmosphere. George Lawrie and his band played every evening. They turned out lovely music, in perfect tempo, to the Quickstep, Slow Foxtrot, and Tango.

A mirrored Globe refracted every colour of the rainbow, as it slowly circled from the ceiling. A long bench at one wall of the dance floor was where the girls would sit chatting to their friends. The boys stood around eyeing the talent.

A balcony upstairs had a small snack bar, serving refreshments and hot pies. There were tables around the balcony, where you could look down on the dancers, while enjoying your snacks.

Once a night there was a ladies' choice, which meant the girls could ask the boys for a dance. The dance would be returned, which was customary and polite. On one such occasion, I went to ask a boy I fancied for a dance. He was a very good dancer and popular with the girls. As I crossed the dance floor, another girl got there before me.

I was a bit embarrassed having to walk back to my seat; however, fate had other plans for me that night. As I was about to walk away, I spied a nice looking young man leaning against one of the pillars. He was tall, with dark wavy hair. I asked him for a dance.

As it turned out, we danced together for the rest of the evening. We spent the next fifty years together and brought up four children.

We often had a laugh about that night. He said he would never have asked me to dance because I was a small girl, and felt more comfortable with taller girls to dance with. I would tell him I did not really fancy him either at the time.

Fate works in mysterious ways.

© Copyright Adelaide Gordon 2004

A Strange Picture   Beatrice Davidson

This is a true story of an experience still fresh in my mind after forty-five years.

In 1959 my husband and I, with our four year old daughter moved from Stirlingshire to Banchory. My husband was in the police force and we transferred north to be nearer to our hometown, Aberdeen.

Housing was quite scarce in those days and we moved into rented accommodation until a police house became available. We were delighted when we heard of a flat to rent in Ramsey Road. The local solicitor showed us around. He was at pains to explain that the flat had been empty for some years, the previous tenant having died. It was with some trepidation that I entered the hallway. To my surprise it was in quite good condition and had a warm, friendly feeling.

There was a small kitchen, a living room with a large, black range, a small bedroom, which would be fine for our daughter, and a large bedroom with a lovely bay window. The view was quite breathtaking. It looked over the village across to the Dee and Scolty. It was far too good just to sleep in. We put a big wardrobe across the black range in the living room and turned the rooms around. When our visitors came from Aberdeen, there was always a rush to have a seat by the window.

One night, several weeks after moving in, my husband came off duty at ten o'clock. He had had a very tiring day and went straight off to bed. A wee while later, trying not to wake him, I went to bed as well. I was lying looking into the darkness, thinking of nothing in particular when I got the most tremendous fright. Someone was showing a cine-film on the wardrobe! I was totally paralysed with fear. I could not move. I am aware that this sounds ridiculous, but it wasn't ridiculous at the time I can tell you.

In this 'film' a young man was helping an older man down the steps outside our flat; he was wearing a fawn raincoat and a brown soft hat. The old man had very distinctive features, a head of curly white hair, and an almost parrot-like nose. What was especially noticeable was his big smile. The young man put a large suitcase into the boot of a grey/blue Morris Minor and they drove off.

When I recovered my faculties I gripped my husband's arm so tightly and stammered out – 'Someone is showing a film on our wardrobe.' He immediately thought I had been dreaming but I had never been asleep. Now, my husband is completely cynical when it comes to anything to do with the supernatural, so I was amazed when he took me seriously. He said he knew by my reactions that what I told him was true. Apparently my face had drained of colour.

The next morning I felt very unsettled and jumpy. I went to see my neighbour. Amy had lived there for a long time. I told her what I had witnessed. She was really quiet, then she said, "You have exactly described John, the man who used to live in your flat. He was such a happy, lovely man. His son took him to live with him when he became too frail to stay alone."

She could not remember what the son's car was like. That evening Amy's son came to see me and he told me that the car was a grey Morris Minor. I was not surprised.

I wish I had some answer. I would love to know if anyone else has had an experience like mine.

Was this a flashback from the past? He was certainly a man who left his mark on people. Did he leave an imprint on a home where he had been very happy?

© Copyright Beatrice Davidson 2004

A Visit to the Maritime Museum   Clarissa Kelly

Visiting the Maritime Museum for me was filled with nostalgia. The memories flooded back to a time when I was surrounded by fish! Or so it seemed.

When I was a child in the 1940s I had three uncles who were trawl fishermen. Two were skippers and one was a deckhand. Suffice to say the skippers made loads of money and the deckhand considerably less.

Just after the war when fruit was scarce and expensive the skipper's children had a plentiful supply, which they delighted in flaunting.

The deckhand uncle, Duncan, was unmarried and lived with his mother, my grandmother in the flat upstairs from where I stayed. He went to sea for about two weeks at a time and was ashore for three days. Being single he could more or less do what he pleased when on land. Mostly he got drunk. In fact he always got drunk. The pocket money he gave my cousin and me depended on how drunk he was. Two shillings and sixpence was normal but on a good day for us when he was very drunk he would give us five shillings. I am embarrassed to say that I would wait to see how drunk he was then ask for our pocket money.

The life at sea was very hard and most trawlermen drank to excess, and who could blame them. The conditions were appalling. Terrible weather, cramped conditions, in boats that resembled rust buckets incapable of surviving the gales of the North Sea, but survive my relatives did. Life was also hard for the womenfolk. My grandmother was constantly knitting big fishermen's jerseys and thick socks out of oily marled wool the weight of which must have been considerable to a woman of her years. The women also had to gut and fillet the fish the men took home as a "fry" and make ends meet when bad weather prevented the boats from going to sea.

I remember as a treat going out to sea in one such trawler. The experience I still remember was one I would not wish to repeat. The boat was skippered by one of my uncles and was only going out to the "bar" to test some equipment. Even so the experience was scary. The boat heaved and rolled and perched up in the wheelhouse, I was convinced it was going to topple over. I was all of ten years old at the time. I still remember the name of the boat it was Jean Stephen.

Fish played an important part in our diet. Fish soup, fish pie, fish cakes, and fried fish. In those days Omelette Arnold Bennet was plain yellow fish omelette. Crabs and prawns were not the delicacy they are today and more or less given away to the fishermen. Fish was our staple food and I hated it. I hated the smell. I hated the bones, I hated the skin, I hated seeing crabs being placed in boiling water whilst still alive. Most of all I hated being told "fish gives you brains, eat it up". It's strange it became my favourite food as an adult.

Not all memories of the fishing industry were unpleasant.

At Christmas time no small stocking was hung up in my house the big fishing socks knitted by my grandmother was the ideal 'stocking' to hang on Christmas Eve. The tangerine and sweeties fitted nicely into the toe of the sock leaving plenty room for presents.

I don't know when the fishing industry started to decline in Aberdeen but before the advent of the oil industry there was a lengthy strike and many trawlermen did not return to the sea. My uncle the deckhand never worked again and descended into alcoholism. He committed suicide and fittingly for a man who spent most of his life at sea, his body was found in the harbour.

As an adult I have further links with the exhibits in the Maritime Museum. My husband originally worked as a joiner in Hall Russell's Shipyard and worked on many of the boats built between 1957-1964 including a luxury yacht for the Johnson & Johnson baby products company. His father worked for many years out of Aberdeen harbour initially as the skipper of the dredger "Hopper" and later on the tug boats.

© Copyright Clarissa Kelly 2004

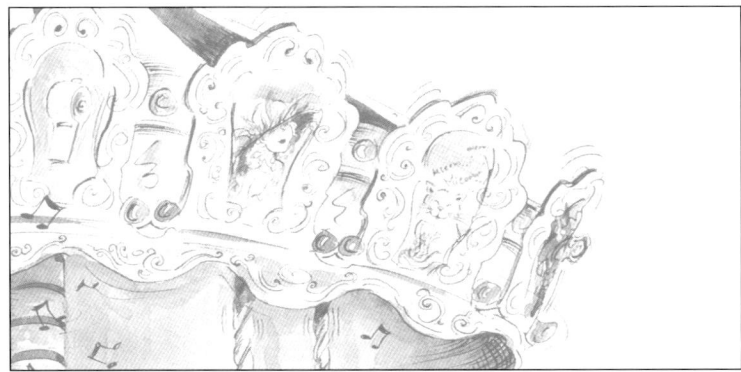

The Wedding Dress   George Crossan

Weddings are special: they ring delightful bells in the hearts of women. No other ceremony carries more wishful expectations of happiness. Marriages are upright and stately. Weddings are downright and cosy. Marriages have rights and obligations; weddings have love and laughter, fun and innocence.

What more encapsulates the complex emotions of a wedding than the wedding dress, itself. With its style, its elegance, its softness, it symbolises the very essence of its function. Simply, it is not to draw attention to itself, but to accentuate the natural attributes of its wearer. Its style may be romantic, but its wearer is never less than beautiful.

Yet, despite its powerfully evocative appeal to the senses, a wedding dress is incomplete without a body, a shape, a form, a smiling face flushed with excitement.

(Photograph by courtesy of Aberdeen Art Gallery)

Thus, an empty wedding dress is unsatisfactory. A vital part is missing: it is made to be worn. Furthermore, this one was bought to be worn. The middle-aged lady who bought it, prudently, perhaps, had a thought that what she herslef admired might find approval in the future from another. Not sadly, perhaps, but unpredictably, that did not happen; and she decided to offer it to the Art Gallery, where it might be displayed for the pleasure of others.

It may be a dress that missed its target; but it can, now, find a wider one. Any woman looking at this dress can fill its outline with her own, imaginatively, depending on her disposition, by formulating in her mind an image of the future, or by recalling, in calm detachment, her past. But all can admire the creative energy of the designer, who captures so much, in modest anonymity.

© Copyright George Crossan 2004

The Common Caul' Edwin Webster

Fit a dose o' caul Ah've hin,
Fairly smoorn wi' it Ah've bin.
A' day lang jist feelin' wabbit,
Jeelie-leggit, girny, crabbit.
Hauchin', hoastin', spreidin' bugs,
Sneezin' fit t' burst m' lugs.
Dirlin'-heidit, greetin'-faced,
Wond'rin' fit bit hurts 'e maist.
Bricht-reed neb an' streamin' een,
Snotters dreepin' on m' sheen.
Pooches fulla sypit hunkies,
Peels t' fleer a dizzin junkies.
Stottin' roon as in a dwam,
Sickin' solace in a dram.
Pictur "Misery in Motion"
Searchin' oot 'e magic potion.
A bucket disna cure, y' kain,
But, Man, it surely soothes 'e pain.
A "common" caul's richt bliddy sair.
Fit hell t' hae a caul 'at's "rare".
Fit a dose o' caul' Ah've hin.
Foo'd y' like a shottie, Min?

© Copyright Edwin Webster 2004

Rock and Roll　　　　　Clarissa Kelly

"Lower that racket!" My father shouted. I hadn't heard him and my mother return from the shops. The racket he referred to was my favourite record, Rock Around The Clock by Bill Haley and the Comets. It was my first record and it cost me three shillings (15p) bought out of my forty-two shilling wages (£2.10) as an office junior. I loved the music but thought Bill Haley with his plump face and kiss curl plastered to his forehead a bit square to be a rock and roll idol.

The year was 1956 I was a teenager sixteen years old, a name coined for young people between thirteen and nineteen years of age. Up until then young people dressed like younger versions of their parents and danced to the same type of music - Frank Sinatra and the Glen Miller band - but all that was about to change. 'Rock and roll' had crossed the Atlantic and hit Britain like a tornado.

According to the national press up and down the country youths were slashing seats in cinemas where an American film "Blackboard Jungle" was being shown. Bill Haley's Rock Around The Clock was the main part of the soundtrack and the alleged cause of the mayhem.

Elvis Presley was next on the scene and he too was greatly criticised by the National Press. He was very different in looks to Bill Haley. Tall, dark and handsome with dark broody eyes and a fantastic voice. He oozed sex appeal. His pelvis thrusting and leg gyrating led to his nickname 'Elvis the Pelvis'. Girls went mad at his concerts and the older generation was convinced we were all doomed and depraved.

In keeping with this new age of music the teenagers wore a new style of clothing. The boys wore Edwardian styled narrow trousers known as 'drainpipes', long draped jackets with velvet collars and a bootlace tie. On their feet they wore thick crepesoled shoes. They were nicknamed 'Teddy Boys'.

The girls had two styles. Below the knee skirts puffed out with numerous underskirts starched with sugar and water to make them stick out (think Sandra Dee in Grease) and long pencil slim straight skirts with a large slit up the back worn with a broad black elastic belt called a 'waspie'.

I don't remember much trouble here in Aberdeen, but things were different in July during the Glasgow Fair when industry shut down for two weeks.

In those days there were no cheap package holidays to Spain and most working people spent their summer holidays at home. Aberdeen was a popular place for Glasgow folk not too far away and it had a beach. Aberdeen was swamped by Glaswegians during those two weeks.

Whigmaleeries: A Word in Your Lug

The Aberdeen girls looked forward to the influx of Glasgow Teddy Boys. They wore the latest gear with suits in midnight blue, mauve and various shades of green; they were always combing their hair, which was either a 'DA' (a ducks rear end) or a Tony Curtis, after a handsome film star at the time. The hair was long on the top and shaped at the back with the front combed onto the forehead like a trunk. Loads of Brylcream was required to keep this style in place. Aberdeen's sea breezes meant constant combing.

I remember on Saturday nights at the Beach Ballroom all the girls would be hanging around waiting for the pubs to close at 9.30pm and the boys to appear. There were no places for the girls to go if they wanted to drink there were only the male dominated type of bars. Female drinking was not encouraged.

Once the bars were shut and the boys had made their way to the dance hall we were outnumbered about three to one and could guarantee being up on the floor at every dance.

Dancing in those days was always to a live band, there were no disc jockeys then. Handbags could be left at your table, no dancing round your handbag. Rock and roll dancing was something else. The energy and skill displayed was spectacular especially by the Glasgow Teddy Boys. Some couples were so good that the other couples would stand aside and look around as the dancing became more and more frenzied.

The Aberdeen Teddy Boys were not too happy about the Glasgow take-over but were a little reticent to get involved in any fracas as the Glaswegians were rumoured to carry weapons and were not slow to use them.

I was never bold enough to get involved with any of the Glasgow lads but I enjoyed watching them strut their stuff, always in group's of three or four. Aberdeen was certainly a little duller when the two weeks were up and the Glasgow Teddy Boy dandies returned home to life in the Glasgow Shipyards for another year.

Girls next time you are shopping in 'International' to the sound of Elvis Presley, tell your Grandma when you get home, she will enjoy her Elvis memories of the 1960's.

© Copyright Clarissa Kelly 2004

Whigmaleeries: A Word in Your Lug

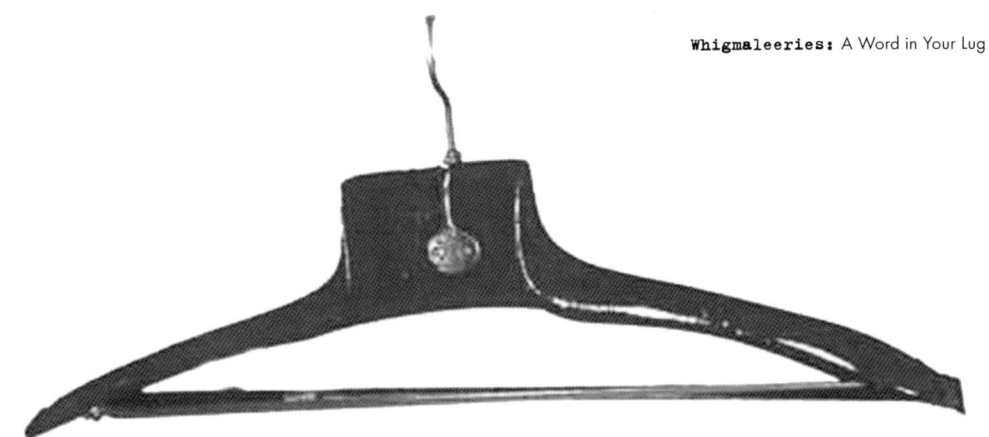

A Coat Hanger   George Crossan

What can I say? Do I describe its admirable shape? Emphasize its quite original structure: its rounded collar-line, its elegant shoulders, its polished woodwork; its unusual, and eminently sensible, metal bar across its middle? These are important features, worthy of a mention, if you are anxious to sell it to someone reluctant to buy it. But I'm not trying to sell it. It doesn't, in fact, belong to me.

If it did, I wouldn't know where to hang it. It looks much too grand, too superior to want to mix it with my lowly born, plastic equivalents (dare I even use such an adjective?). My hangers would feel patronized and insecure in such well mannered, distinguished company. The types that hang about in my wardrobe are a rowdy, squabbling bunch, who fall about and slide all over the place, without even an excuse me.

Nevertheless, if I were truly candid, I would have to mention that I do own, already, a much-treasured coat hanger, marked (believe me!) in gold: 'Crombie, est. 1805'! It even has a coat of arms. Our fine-quality model can't beat that! With luck and guidance, I might be able to pass it on to the Art Gallery one day, to lie there, smugly and contentedly, a companion to our resident model (in its cardboard box), warmly cuddled in the bosoms of their feminine wrappings.

I can even boast of some other makes: a strong, well-shaped DAK and a stylish Pierre Cardin. (Because I'm being frank, I have to confess to a MAKRO and a NEXT – but they're tucked away at the back of my wardrobe).

My Crombie, DAK and Pierre Cardin, however, possess extra qualities, not enjoyed by our collector's model: each one of them carries personal associations that give them a unique, emotional appeal, even a sort of celebrity status, denied to their ancient competitor.

For instance, fifty years ago, before I married, I counselled my intended wife that, if she had an ambition to possess a particular expensive item of clothing, she should buy it there and then - otherwise, I knew, she would have a long time to wait for its fulfilment. She bought a fur coat, quite fashionable and acceptable in those days. I bought a Crombie overcoat, down to my ankles, so heavy it needed a chain to hang it on a peg. I still have it; a bit threadbare now at the edges, but rapidly becoming a family legacy. The DAK came to me with an out-of-the-ordinary sports jacket, a singular, self-indulgent treat after graduation. Later, when I was caught up in television, its bold pattern was so dominant that cameramen used to line up their lenses on it, prior to transmission. It was almost as important as the established Test Card! (These were early days, before the luxury of video recording). And the Pierre Cardin? Well, I make use of that example to boast that I once had a waistline that any man would have been proud of! I still have the suit (and the hanger) but, sadly, not the waist.

Thus, old clothes hangers, like many other ancient bits and pieces, may be admired – and countless often are - for their appearance, for their structure, for their antiquity and for their rarity. But their value to the mere collector, or observer, may never be quite the same as their subjective worth to their original owner. Clothes, people may say, maketh the man; but man and his memories may sometimes maketh the hanger!

© Copyright George Crossan 2004

The Worst Night of the Blitz April 1943   Adelaide Gordon

I recall the night back in 1943; I was ten years old. My mother and I went to visit my Aunt in George Street; I was being fitted for a dress being made by my Aunt who was a seamstress. I was standing on the table as my mother and Aunt pinned the hem. It was a pretty dress; I was to be a flower girl at a cousin's wedding. That was the chief reason we were out in the evening, I don't think my parents ever went out in the evening during the blitz.

Aberdeen was heavily bombed during the war. The siren could sound at any time. That evening the siren went, within a few minutes, there was a terrific noise of planes flying very low over the buildings.

Suddenly there was a session of loud bangs. The whole house shook, pictures hung askew on the walls. I remember some plaster cracked on the ceiling showering us with fine dust. We were terrified, we at first crouched under the big table in the middle of the room. There was a lot of noise in the streets as people were shouting. A.R.P. wardens were giving instructions for everyone to take cover in their shelters, which were in most back gardens.

It seemed an age before things became quieter. We emerged from under the table. My Aunt made some tea, soon after the all clear went. My mother was anxious to get home; knowing my father would be deeply concerned for our safety. We eventually went out into the street, heading for home. It was very dark, as it was the blackout; there were no streetlights. I was amazed that the sky was bright orange with black smoke billowing over the top of some houses a short distance away.

This may have been the fact that Broadford Works was bombed. George Street and all areas around were bombed - Catherine Street, Fraser Place, Charles Street. The pavements were littered with broken glass; the trams were stopped, the lines being damaged. We had a long walk home, past Woodside onto Middlefield where we lived at the time.

I remember I stumbled over some rubble and glass and cut my hand. It had been a long night and being so young I was getting very tired having to walk so far. My mother quickly tied a handkerchief round the wound and we proceeded to head for home. We had walked the length of George Street and were heading for Great Northern Road.

There was quite a way to go. We could still here the far off rat a tat of machine gun fire as our spitfires chased the enemy planes out to sea. My father was so relieved to see us safe and well. My small wound was washed and bandaged and I was put to bed. I fell asleep, my parents sat up till what was left of the night.

We didn't have air raid shelters at that time. Most of the neighbours collected together in the bottom flat of the tenement where we lived. They may have felt more comforted being all in the one place together.

© Copyright Adelaide Gordon 2004

The Fabulous Fifties   Beatrice Davidson

After the deprivations of the war, the Fifties were wonderful. I was sixteen and had just started work in a solicitor's office in Union Street. The regime was draconian and I was always in trouble. I left there to work with an engineering company. It suited me much better – all those men – and I was such a flirt!

From Jimmy Donald's dance hall in North Silver Street I graduated to Beach Ballroom and the Palais. I cannot remember if there were any bars in these ballrooms, I certainly cannot remember any fighting or drunkenness. The big bands - Joe Loss, Ted Heath, Oscar Rabin – all appeared quite regularly. The queue for the tickets stretched along the prom.

The 'New Look' had arrived by then. My mother made me a circular taffeta skirt. I had the obligatory paper nylon petticoat – well soaked in sugar and water to achieve the stiff effect. With my first pair of nylons and wedge heel shoes, I felt the bee's knees. It was certainly a step up from my party dress made from a nylon parachute!

National Service was a real nuisance. No sooner had you started a romance, than the blow fell and off they went to the RAF, Army or Navy for two years. You promised to stay true, but – well – two years were a long time!

The Fifties were a life-changing time for me. I left school, started work, got married, left home and had my first child, a daughter. I also moved house five times. My husband was in the Police Force and in those days no one was left in a village or small town too long. I feel the thinking behind it was that you would become too friendly with the locals.

On one station we were posted to, we occupied the station officer's house. A door in the living room led directly into the cell passageway. It was quite usual to be sitting in the living room and hear some drunk vomiting in the cells.

As there were no policewomen at the station it fell to me to search any female prisoners. One night three women, a mother and two daughters were run in. They were the real McCoy – tinkers from the Highlands. They had been drinking Cherry Blossom boot polish dissolved in boiling water and they sang Gaelic all night. When I took them a cup of tea the mother asked if I would look in her bag for her stomach powders! Would that have been a side-effect of the boot polish?

Of course there were the regulars – I got to know some of them quite well. To the extent in fact that I knew not to give one man Empire biscuits as the icing upset him! I was paid 3/- per meal. It was more economical to serve them what we were having. Many Sunday they were given roast beef and trimmings. We had lots of laughs and there was a great camaraderie with the other policemen and their wives.

Maybe it is just my imagination, but I feel people were friendlier and kinder to each other back then. Or am I just looking back through rose-coloured glasses?

© Copyright Beatrice Davidson 2004

Whigmaleeries: A Word in Your Lug

Slum Clearance   Clarissa Kelly

"We are getting a new house!" My mother waved the Council Housing Department letter excitedly in the air. Her face filled with wonder as she babbled on about new furniture and carpets and curtains claiming that our furniture was too old and scruffy to move to a brand new house. I did not share her enthusiasm I did not want to leave the neighbourhood and my friends.

The year was 1953 I was thirteen years old. A massive building programme was in progress in an attempt to re-house the post war population into decent accommodation. The house we lived in was declared a slum. It consisted of two rooms, shared by my family, two adults and three children. My parents slept in a bed in the kitchen, and myself brother and sister shared the other room. There was a sink in the kitchen but no hot water. The toilet was outside.

At the back of our house was an old yard, the remains of a coal store and stables, which my grandparents had run as a coal merchants business before the war. With their sons off fighting the business had floundered and the premises became derelict.

My father had always considered himself as a 'man of the land' and in an attempt to make our surroundings more pleasing, manufactured a garden. He dug up the cobbles in the yard and laid some top soil and planted flowers. He painted the wall backing the garden with whitewash, added a small fence which he painted green and white to complete the transformation. It was beautiful. In the summer time huge roses climbed the whitewashed wall, their perfume heady in the hot humid days.

He was not so successful at joinery work. To add to our garden he bought two white fantail pigeons and decided to make a wooden house for them. Making it he accidentally sawed part of the chair he was using for support. Once completed and painted green and white to match the fence, the birds were installed and placed outside in the garden. However the first time he let the birds out they flew off and never returned, preferring the company of the local "doos" (pigeons).

The outside toilet was also white-washed. It was a great place to spend time with your friends trading secrets whilst seated on the toilet. Yes the 'lavvy' was an important refuge with houses so small.

Inside the house was a different story. The rooms were small and cramped; the plaster behind the wallpaper was lumpy and crumbled. Mice could be heard running inside the walls and could often be seen scurrying about the floor. In the bedroom I shared with my brother and sister was a cupboard which held the gas meter. The bedroom had a constant smell of gas.

The day came to visit the new house. A journey by tramcar to the Bridge of Dee, a walk over the bridge and up a path to a street over looking the Stonehaven Road took us to a row of granite houses. We counted along to number thirty-eight and climbed the steps to the side entrance. There was a large garden back and front. Once inside we children ran about from room to room like headless chickens. Three bedrooms upstairs, a living room, kitchen and bathroom downstairs. The house was bigger than the whole tenement we had left.

Living there had it's good points, a bedroom to myself, hot running water and everything new but with both parents now working to furnish the house and pay the larger rent meant that things were not so cushy for me. After school housework had to be done and furniture polished. I could never understand why every house had a sideboard made of highly polished walnut wood complete with drop down front that revealed a cocktail cabinet containing scrolled glass and a pink fluorescent strip light, but no cocktails. I cannot imagine many working class men coming home from work and having a cocktail.

My memories of the old house are of cosy nights in front of the fire, the sweet smell of roses, long summer days collecting their petals to make perfume, searching for caterpillars in the Thom Thumbs, and of earnest conversations in the lavvy. The terror of the mice running about the room and the over powering smell of gas and the crumbling walls has diminished with time as unpleasant memories often do. The new house always felt like the new house. I have no fond memories of it perhaps at thirteen my memories had already been embedded in the formative years living in the slum.

© Copyright Clarissa Kelly 2004

Whigmaleeries: A Word in Your Lug

Safety Razor   George Crossan

It lies on its back in a leather-clad rectangular box, a dumb witness of a bygone age, a relic in fact not just of a person, but of a generation. Its work is not quite done: it is still usable, although discarded. Sadly, razors like this, beautifully machined with engineering precision, have been dumped, unwanted nowadays, by those who prefer more efficient – but plastic – counterfeits.

The safety razor first appeared in the toilet bag of the man-about-town at the beginning of the 20th century. The first model was produced by an American, King C. Gillette, in 1903. It replaced the larger, open ('cut-throat') razor, a lethal, dangerous, cutting implement, if inexpertly used. It was an overnight success. The main feature of the safety-razor was the provision of a guard which smoothed out the skin before cutting the unwanted hair, so reducing the risk of wounding or bleeding the user. Its popularity was increased by the fact that the blades used were replaceable, disposable and cheap. Numerous versions flooded the market in the 1950s.

This particular model is an up-market version, a Valet, with a more expensive, more efficient blade that could be re-sharpened by stropping it on a leather strap, tidily stored, here, under the razor. A third compartment contains extra blades.

Our mind dwells for a moment on its possible user. In its day, a Valet was more expensive than some other makes. The extra blades and leather strap, would add to its comprehensiveness. From its design, it was surely meant to be carried in a business case, a weekend toilet bag, or in something similar - its ornate container would be ineffectual in a bathroom cabinet. Being encased in a compact, leather-clad box adds an attractive, de luxe, quality to the owner's choice, even as its capacity to have its blades re-sharpened could indicate the thriftiness of a man of means. The polished elegance of its construction suggests the aesthetics of a man of taste. Taken as a whole, it could have been the choice of a person with an urbane and discriminatory sense of values.

This shaver might tell other tales, if it were not, by its nature, such a mute observer.

© Copyright George Crossan 2004

Whigmaleeries: A Word in Your Lug

Once Upon a Time...

Local Enterprise
Edwin Webster

Followers of the original series of "Star Trek", charting the adventures of the crew of the Starship Enterprise, may perhaps remember one particular episode in which Chief Engineer Scott, or Scotty as he is popularly known, nostalgically recalled a pub-crawl he went on in Aberdeen in his younger days. Many years later in A.D 2004 in fact, by a strange twist of fate, Scotty and Captain Kirk found themselves in Aberdeen, when the Enterprise became caught up in a time warp. Realising that the time warp they were caught up in was "user friendly" and would be only of short duration, Kirk took the opportunity to transport himself and Mr Scott down to Aberdeen so that together they could revisit the scenes of Scotty's youthful escapade. Jim Kirk, who a few minutes earlier had been sitting on the bridge, contemplating his navel and thinking that the new corset he wore was far too tight, suddenly found himself flung into the hurly-burly of a boozy night-out in Aberdeen. His visit to the city happened to coincide with the busiest time of a frantically busy Saturday, during "Happy Hour" at many licensed premises, when the revolting young natives were indeed at their most revolting.

The pair were beamed down to the junction of King Street and West North Street, the starting point of Scotty's original booze-fest. Ten minutes later, they stood at the top of Queen Street and Broad Street, with Scotty shaking his head in disbelief and complaining to Kirk, in that unmistakable accent of his which indisputably placed his roots in the Connemara area of the Granite City: "I dinna believe it, Cap'n. They've torn doon all thon pubs – The Hairy Bar, The Volunteer, Banks O' Ythan, The Artillery Arms – even the pawn shop's gone! We'll hae to go to the Castlegate and start fae there."

So their pub-crawl began in Castle Street, where Scotty managed to raise some money by selling a gold ring. This was a hectic night in the city pubs and clubs, and a number of hen parties, stag nights and fancy-dress affairs were taking place, besides the customary binge drinking. Kirk and Scotty fitted into the scene extremely well, dressed as they were in their Starfleet uniforms; they were actually taken for lookalikes of themselves! This led to them being stood a considerable number of drinks, a considerable number indeed, because "Happy Hour" meant a double for the price of a single. In no time at all, the pair were very much in the party mood; they moved uptown and arrived in Windmill Brae, the heart of clubland. As things were really swinging, and there seemed a real possibility that the two might become separated, they agreed that if this happened, each would use his personal communicator to beam up to the Enterprise in his own time.

As a result of this agreement, Scotty came aboard the Enterprise before Capt. Kirk, long before. His beaming smile, the reek of whisky and the unsteadiness of his gait clearly showed that he had had a very good time. Kirk arrived much later, and after spending a short time on the bridge, was admitted to the sick-bay. Spock assumed command, and the Enterprise having been released from the time-warp, ordered a new course to be plotted, and sent the vessel into the next stage of its mission.

The following day Kirk appeared on the bridge, looking distinctly unwell. He sat down heavily and groaned. The principal members of the crew were assembled: Mr Spock, Dr McCoy, Mr Sulu, Chekhov, Scotty and the leading female member of the navigation team, the stunning Uhura, object of a million male fantasies. Kirk peered blearily through bloodshot eyes and grimaced.

"Right," he said, "tell me all about last night. I can hardly remember a thing except that I think the locals quite liked me. They said they thought I was absolutely stocious."

"But Cap'n," interjected Scotty, "that's local lingo for being very drunk."

"Oooh," groaned Kirk, "I can't understand how I got so drunk, I was only drinking girders – a local soft drink called Iron Brew or something."

"Aye, Skipper," replied Scotty, "but there was a double vodka in every one."

Kirk groaned again. "But you transported me back up again ok didn't you?"

"Aye Cap'n," retorted Scotty, "I spoke to you myself, that's when I realised you were bleezing – that's another local word for very drunk. Your instructions to me were 'Steam me up Botty', then when you materialised, you were reelin' around like a demented Hielander. And you were wearin a pair o' lace panties on your heid. Black frilly ones."

Kirk looked gloomingly at Scotty, then at McCoy, and asked the doctor, "How did I end up in sick-bay Bones?"

"Well Jim," replied McCoy carefully, "you went a bit haywire. You were chasing Uhura around the flight deck yelling "Hey! Melons! Melons! Melons! Gimme some of those melons!" When Mr Sulu tried to intervene, you kicked him in the nuts. You kept shouting: 'Melons! Melons! Gimme! Gimme!' Eventually I had to tranquillise you and we carried you into sick-bay and put you in the next bed to Mr Sulu."

For the umpteenth time, Kirk groaned. Although it is a well-known fact that Vulcans have little sense of humour, Dr McCoy could have sworn that Spock's lower lip twitched slightly, and was sure that this was the Vulcan equivalent of a belly laugh.

On the Monday after the aforementioned weekend, the following headline appeared in the 'Aberdeen Observer': **"Mystery Reveller disappears into thin air.** The accompanying

Whigmaleeries: A Word in Your Lug

report revealed how dozens of party goers had witnessed a male, dressed as Captain Kirk of the Enterprise, wearing a pair of black knickers on his head and clutching a mobile phone, stagger into the middle of Union Street, then simply vanish. A police spokesman indicated that no trace had been found of the missing man but that enquiries were on going. An unofficial source revealed that the authorities doubted the credibility of the witnesses – the phrase, "they were a' blootered", was used.

The manager of nearby licensed premises hinted that perhaps the witness had indulged rather freely and that their perception had been impaired; he had seen one Superman, two Batmen, one Spiderman, Wonder Woman, an Incredible Hulk, several Hobbits, but no Captain Kirk.

No woman was bold enough to report the loss of a pair of black, frilly knickers; nor any man.

© Copyright Edwin Webster 2004

The Dark at the Bottom of the Stairs   Adelaide Gordon

Laura awoke with a start. It was pitch dark. She thought it must be the middle of the night. She was about to drop off to sleep again, when an unfamiliar sound coming from downstairs startled her. Holding her breath, heart pounding, she thought someone might be in the house.

Living alone, since her husband passed away, made Laura nervous, especially at night-time. She reached for the bed light and sat up, leaning against her pillows. Looking at the clock it was ten past three. She called out her husband's name thinking it may scare off any intruders.

Her imagination began to run riot. What if someone was creeping up the stairs? Should she phone her next door neighbour? Laura decided not to disturb them for now. Her cat Mini often took a mad turn at night, chasing her toys. Maybe she had knocked over something in the lounge.

There was another sound as she listened intently. Deciding to get out of bed, Laura crept to the top of the landing. Switching on the lights, she noticed that the hallway was still in darkness. It must be a fuse she thought, she would have to remember to change the bulb in the morning. Halfway down the stairs, still a bit wary, she peered into the darkened hallway. She gasped, as a tall black figure seemed to be leaning against the wall. She shrank back, ready to dash back upstairs to the safety of her room and call for help.

It suddenly dawned on her, the coat stand with her own black winter cloak, had given the impression there was someone standing there. She sat down on the stairs; relieved no one was in her house. Gathering her thoughts, she decided to check the lounge to see if Mini had broken anything or knocked anything over. Everything seemed to be in order, Laura was not aware of what was lurking behind the sofa.

Now wide-awake, she decided to make herself a cup of tea. Her cat, thinking it was time for her breakfast, started to pester Laura for some food. To get a bit of peace, she decided to feed her. She reached for the tin of cat food.

Suddenly an intruder rushed from the lounge. He grabbed Laura from behind and encircled an arm around her neck. Shocked by the assault, she felt dizzy, almost passing out. Her cat darted past the attacker, which distracted him. He loosened his grip on Laura, which enabled her to twist her body away giving her a chance to whack him on the head with the tin she was still holding.

He drew back, clutching his face. Laura dashed for the front door; her hands trembled as she fumbled with the lock. The door flew open. She ran down the path, shouting for help.

Whigmaleeries: A Word in Your Lug

Lights went on as her neighbours heard her calling out. They were astonished to see Laura fleeing from her home in the middle of the night. They came out of their houses to help her. The culprit came rushing out of her home and was tackled by young James next door, a strapping rugby player.

Laura had left a window open in her kitchen. That is where the thief had come into the house. He did not have enough time to steal, being interrupted by Laura. Thinking back, she wondered what might have happened to her if Mini did not ask for some food. Who would have thought a tin of cat food would have been a weapon to defend oneself?

© Copyright Adelaide Gordon 2004

Whigmaleeries: A Word in Your Lug

Hunter's Moon   Edwin Webster

It is a little-known fact, that in the last decade of Queen Victoria's reign, Sherlock Holmes and Dr. John Watson visited Aberdeen at the urgent behest of the Lord Provost; summoned north by the first citizen to locate his missing chain of office. The Provost entreated the great detective to conduct his investigation with the utmost discretion, in order that the Council avoid the embarrassment of public humiliation and derision should details of the mislaid regalia leak out. Consequently, the case was not recorded by Dr. Watson, so no first-hand account exists. Thus, the following narrative is cobbled together from fragments of information, gossip and rumour, which have circulated in the city over the course of a century or more. No responsibility is taken for its accuracy.

What seems clear is that early in his investigation, Holmes absolved the Lord Provost, Councillors and staff of any direct involvement in the disappearance of the chain; some were guilty of stupidity and some of inebriation but these were expected and commonplace infractions of the ilk.

Holmes quickly concluded that he was looking for a woman in connection with the affair. Hence, cherchez la femme. Following this line of enquiry, it was in a docklands hostelry that Sherlock Holmes, master of disguise, masqueraded as a lady of the night (and most fetchingly too, by all accounts). Here, whilst sipping a large glass of gin, he was indecently assaulted by a foreign sailor and a fracas ensued. Soon a free-for-all developed, involving soldiers, sailors and members of the public and order was not restored until the constabulary had cracked many skulls with their truncheons. In the mêlée, Fittie Fanny (alias Sherlock Holmes) contrived to slip off into the darkness unnoticed, and in possession of a vital clue.

Soon, after meeting up with Watson and changing clothes, the pair were swift afoot and beating a path to the Gallowgate and to the address Holmes obtained prior to the disturbance in the public house. What occurred next is shrouded in mystery, but what is certain is that a local worthy was caught in a compromising position and was somehow accidentally shot in the buttocks by Dr. Watson. This unfortunate gentleman was borne away on a stretcher, face down, his head covered with a blanket to preserve his anonymity. The female in the case was led away, heavily-veiled. The Provost's regalia was recovered from its hiding-place and restored to that dignitary sans pomp or ceremony.

The chain had been stolen with blackmail in mind. The lady in question, having engineered a liaison with a leading public figure, pumped him for information, but in such a skilful way that he was unaware that he was a mere pawn in her machinations. She carried out the robbery herself, alone and unaided. She was biding her time before sending a demand to the Provost, confident that he would pay up rather than allow the matter to become public. She reckoned without Sherlock Holmes. The mystery woman was taken to the railway station, handed a one-way ticket and banished from Scotland forever. She faded from sight but eventually re-surfaced in Berlin, married to a wealthy Prussian aristocrat. During the Great War, she exercised considerable influence over the Kaiser, and when her image appeared in The Times, Holmes was heard to mutter darkly: "A pity Watson plugged the wrong party."

Apropos her companion on that fateful night, it was inevitable that word would leak out concerning the nature and cause of his painful injury. Stories quickly spread, and for the rest of his life, the hapless victim was referred to as Bullseye Bill. This nickname was whispered wherever and whenever he showed his face. Cheap jokes abounded. When he took his seat at a public event, spiteful officials took great delight in providing him with a chair having the minimum of padding. Such treatment caused his premature retirement from public life.

It is reported that, just before he left the city, Holmes called on the Lord Provost in his private chambers and delivered this parting shot: "In the course of my travels around the globe, I have witnessed many wondrous sights, natural and man-made; seen splendid cities and towns too numerous to mention, and enjoyed great hospitality and warm fellowship; these images will live long in the memory; Aberdeen will not be among them." Holmes vowed never to return to the Granite City; the quality of cocaine in the area was to his liking, but the inclement weather got right up his nose.

© Copyright Edwin Webster 2004

Eckie's Ghost   anne flann

Sitting quietly in the corner of the bar, the figure of a tall man sat on the barstool, resting back against the faded beige wall. Head bent wearily down, the gaunt face, weathered yet pale, seemed lost in contemplation. Before him on the gleaming surface stood a shot glass of amber whisky.

The proprietors Maggie and Hector busied themselves, filling beer glasses, greeting customers as they filled the tiny room at tables and some approached the bar to chat with the popular couple. None sat near the bent figure at the end.

A young lass scurried back and forth taking orders from the jovial handful of men, bandying remarks with a pert toss of blonde curls and a sweet smile on her face. The men raised heads as a figure entered from the lounge bar of the small inn. A tall man, clad in jeans and sweater, entered a bit hesitantly, ducking his head against the low beamed ceiling. He made his way to the bar and was about to sit at the end, but Maggie cried "Join the others here, sir. That's a right draughty corner you've chosen." With a wide grin the young man, joined the couple at the bar, thrusting out his hand, "Name's Ken. Staying here a couple of days. From the States on a short break." The two men shook hands and the stranger said "Join me for a drink?" To which the pair replied, "Maybe later – young Jeanie's just put down our meal at the table." The redolent smell of good Scotch Broth permeated Ken's taste buds. "Gee, that smells good, guess I'll have some of that," he turned to Maggie. "I'll have a portion of game pie too, Ma'am – your husband Hector says it's the best in Scotland." Hector standing filling glasses, grinned. "You'll not be sorry, sir. Did you find the church, then? It's a bonny wee kirk and goes back many years." Ken nodded. He'd been on the go since early – he'd found the hotel bed just a bit on the short side for his height and hadn't slept that well.

Seated at the small table, he tucked into the good Scottish fare hungrily. Around him the other men speculated what brought this stranger to such a remote area at this time of year – it was a bit late for the usual tourist. Finished, a few returned to the bar for a blether and a dram. None sat near the lone man, still nursing his small whisky.

Ken, replete, joined the now depleted bar, but noted his earlier companions and begged them to have that drink with him. The two happily accepted and they blethered for a while, telling tales of the area, learning that the tall stranger came from Boston and was here doing research on sabbatical from College.

Later they took their leave and gradually the small bar emptied. Ken remained over his Grouse whiskey, assuring Hector that it had been on TV he'd noticed the name – "That's a great ad – I just love that bird, it's so funny." Hector smiled, "But you should try a pure malt, Ken. Here, have one on the house?" Ken grinned his thanks and tentatively sipped the peaty malt.

"Why don't you offer one on my tab to the old fellow at the end there – seems a lonely sort." Maggie and Hector exchanged an odd look. "That's real kind of you," Maggie said in a soft voice. "I'll ask him later – he tends to be a loner." They all glanced down to the corner. The old man raised his head, uplifted the glass, placed the empty glass on the polished bar and was gone.

Ken, bewildered, cried, "Where the hell has he gone?" The couple exchanged looks. "Well, it's a sad story," Hector said. "You see, we didn't realise you saw him till you offered the drink. Old Eckie died there at the bar some three years ago. We thought he'd fallen asleep and the last barmaid went over to waken him, and found he'd just slipped away. Gave her an awful turn that did. She left soon after. Well, every year since, on that same night, he sits there. We placed a drink there in commemoration the following year, for he was a fine old man, and he's appeared every year since. Some see him, some don't."

"Gee that's some story," Ken shook his head in wonder. "Guess I never really believed in ghosts. What was the old boy's name?" "Old Eckie," Maggie said "Well, his real name was Alec Donald, he was an estate worker from a boy. Then when the old Laird died, the estate was sold, no heirs you see, lost at the last war. The new owner pensioned him off. Guess he just pined away, poor man. Gave his life to the old Laird. Took to the bottle after that. Just used to come in and sit over his whiskey, never bothered a soul. We loved the old chap, which is why we made a sort of tradition of the shot of whisky on the day he died."

She looked at Ken's face. His expression was shocked. "My name's Ken Donald. I came up here to research my father's family. His father came from around here – name of Alec Donald."

© Copyright Anne Flann 2004

Show A Leg!   Edwin Webster

In 1947, Evaline went on holiday to London. A spinster in her early thirties, Evaline had served in the Land Army during the war and afterwards suffered a serious illness, being hospitalised for several months. She reckoned that a fortnight in London, spent with her brother and his family, would do her a power of good and speed a full recovery.

Although still pockmarked by bomb-sites, the capital city was beginning to rise from the ruins of war. There were squads of workmen everywhere, either clearing away debris or erecting new buildings on empty sites. Jobs were available for all that wanted them, but, as ever, there were those who weren't prepared to work, certainly not for a working wage; and then there were those that no employer would hire under any circumstances. Some of those not in gainful employment engaged in criminal activities, as members of gangs, organised groups which did big "jobs", like post office or bank robberies, or emptied warehouses or storage areas of valuable goods which could be sold on the "black" market.

Then there were the spivs. The dictionary defines a spiv as; "a man, often characterised by flashy dress, who makes a living by illicit or unscrupulous dealings." They were basically small-time crooks, who sold items out of suitcases on street corners. The articles they "flogged" were generally stolen, counterfeit or defective. At the first sight of a "rozzer", the spiv would hastily close up his suitcase and "do a runner."

A well-known music-hall performer, Arthur English, made a steady living from portraying a spiv onstage. He wore a narrow waisted suit with extravagantly padded shoulders, a trilby hat and had a pencil-line moustache. The mowser was the hallmark of the spiv, as was the gaudy tie he wore around his neck.

During the war, Americans stationed in Britain had a major impact on British life and culture. They provided many items unavailable to Britons, but readily obtainable to themselves through their own servicemen's stores. These included chocolate, chewing gum, American cigarettes, luxury tinned goods, and the commodity most sought-after by womenfolk – the nylon stocking! British women went crazy for nylons. Before these appeared, stockings were made from wool, lisle, or silk. There was such a shortage of sheer stockings that women would use cold tea to stain their legs, then get a friend to use an eyebrow pencil to draw a line down the back of their calves to simulate a seam. Spivs very quickly cottoned on to the attraction of nylon stockings and used it to their advantage.

Meanwhile, Evaline did her tourist trips around "The Big Smoke"; saw the major sights and absorbed the sounds and smells of the city. Near the street market in Petticoat Lane, she encountered a spiv selling nylons at five shillings (25p) a pair out of a battered suitcase.

Whigmaleeries: A Word in Your Lug

She listened to his patter: "Genuine American nylons, love. Straight off the boat this morning. You won't find better anywhere. Not even in New York. All the best people wear 'em. Only five bob a pair, missus."

Evaline was hooked. Five shillings was a fair sum but she willingly shelled out the cash to get her hands on a pair of nylons. She couldn't wait to get back to her digs and try them on. Her fingers fumbled with the cellophane wrapper as she tried to rip it open. Finally she got hold of the new stockings and put them on. Alas, disappointment awaited and her wailing was heard abroad: "My God! I've been swicked! The seams are up the front!"

© Copyright Edwin Webster 2004

The Purple Hat [1]   Clarissa Kelly

Maggie woke early and looked at the clock it was 6.30am time to get up. She was tired it had been a long and disruptive night. Bill's coughing seemed worse but he was now settled into a light sleep. She could hear the rasp of his laboured consumptive breathing as he lay beside her.

She sat up in bed and looked at the kitchen from the bed recess. The fire was dead and had to be cleaned and lit. It was difficult to prise herself from the warm bed but she forced her feet onto the cold bare linoleum and reached for a cardigan to cover her shoulders and set about her daily routine.

Once the fire was lit and the breakfast made she went into the other of their two rooms to waken her daughter Emily. She stood momentarily and looked at the still sleeping child, her little mouth slightly open, her hair damp on her forehead. She loved her so much her only child what would happen to them. Bill's health was deteriorating rapidly he was confined to sitting at the fireside with his laboured breathing and incessant coughing. Emily had seen flashes of red on the cloths her dad surreptitiously spat into following the coughing bouts, but her mother did not discuss her father's health with her. She always appeared cheery.

With Emily off to school and a supply of coal in the skuttle for Bill to keep the fire going Maggie set off to work.

She left the tenement flat and set off for the West End of the town where she had managed to get a skivvying job to a well-known solicitor, his wife and daughter. The house was large and the work hard. The family more or less ignored her other than to tell her what needed to be done. There was a cook but she ignored Maggie as well, looking down on the skivvy from her superior position.

Maggie walked the same route to the big house every day passing several shops on the way. As she came to her favourite, Kays Hat Shop, she saw the most beautiful hat she had ever seen. It was a child's hat set bang in the middle of the window in full splendour. It was purple velour trimmed all the way round the brim with ostrich feathers dyed the same shade of purple. There was a delicate black elastic band attached at each side to fit under the chin. It was beautiful. Maggie thought of the hat on her daughter's head. The colour would show off her blonde curls and compliment her blue grey eyes it was made for her. Maggie decided she would have to get it for Emily's birthday. She hurried on her way with her thoughts in turmoil. How could she afford to buy the hat.

Over the following months Maggie checked the shop window for the hat every day relieved by it's appearance until one morning it was gone. Maggie was devastated. Who could have bought it. She did not have to wait long to find out.

Maggie continued on her way to the big house. Her heart was heavy and she dragged her feet there was only one thing on her mind, the purple ostrich feather hat. It had become an obsession with her. She had scrimped and saved from other meagre wages for her daughter to have something beautiful in her life.

When she arrived at the house and entered the hallway she saw a cardboard hatbox on the hall table. Kay's Hat Shop was written in bold letters on the side of the gaily-coloured box. Without hesitating Maggie lifted the lid her breathing shallow and her heart thumping. Inside was the purple ostrich feather hat. Emily's hat. What was it doing here? Maggie replaced the lid picked up the hatbox and walked out of the house.

She half walked and half ran back to her own home holding firmly onto the hatbox. She arrived breathless. Bill, sitting by the fire, looked up surprised to see his wife home. He was too ill to notice her demeanour, wild eyed and excited. Anticipating his wonder Maggie tried to calm down, "I got the day off, the mistress thought I looked unwell". She concealed the hatbox as she spoke.

All day she waited for Emily to come home from school. What had she done she had never stolen anything in her life, what had come over her. These thoughts raced through her mind. How was she going to explain the hat?

When Emily arrived home she found her father sitting in his usual chair. He looked weaker; he did not look up as his daughter came running in. Her mother seemed different but Emily thought it was because she was worried about her father.

"I've got something to give you Emily, it is an early present for your eleventh birthday". Maggie handed Emily the hatbox. The little girl had never seen such a gaily-coloured box before, she opened the lid and gasped as she saw nestling in tissue paper a purple hat. She took it out gently and placed it on her head. The ostrich feathers moving gently in the draughty room. Maggie thought her daughter was beautiful standing there with the hat perched on her blonde curls. "This is the best present I have ever had, I am going to keep it forever."

© Copyright Clarissa Kelly 2004

The Purple Hat [2]   Clarissa Kelly

"Becky put away the toys, your mother is here". Becky heard her grandmother shout as she played with the box of dressing up clothes. She put the clothes back into the box and went into the kitchen where her grandmother was preparing the evening meal. "You've got the purple hat on your head" said her grandmother. "Yes I know. I love this hat can I take it home with me?" "Please Grandma." Becky said in her best wheedling voice, guaranteed to get her own way. "Well, just for a few days, if you take things home there will be nothing left for you to dress up in when you come to see me".

Becky's mother came into the house, and chatted with Becky's grandmother over a cup of coffee. Becky preened herself in the hall mirror holding her head this way and that. She loved the hat. It was purple velvet with lovely feathers all round the brim. Some of the feathers were slightly bedraggled and hung down over her forehead tickling her face.

All the way home in the car she sat with the hat firmly on her head and once home she placed it gently on her dressing table while she had her tea.

Later when Becky went to bed she couldn't resist trying on the purple hat again. She sat admiring herself in the mirror then as she looked she saw her reflection change to that of another girl of about her same age. This girl was wearing the purple hat. She had long blonde curly hair and blue grey eyes. She looked very sad. Her clothes were weird they looked like the clothes worn by people in Becky's history book.

As Becky looked the sad looking girl spoke. She gazed straight into Becky's eyes. "Hello" she said. Becky was astonished. She looked behind herself and around the room not knowing what she was looking for. "Hello" she answered in a faltering voice. "Who are you? Why are you so sad? What is your name? Where did you get the hat you're wearing? I know that hat".

The girl in the mirror continued to speak. She said her name was Emily, and she was an only child. She said that her father had died and her mother had been taken away. She was in an orphanage as she had no other living relatives who could look after her. She said she was so unhappy. "Why was your mother taken away?" Asked Becky. The little girl spoke in a trembling voice and told her story.

She said she was eleven years old and as she had said earlier her father had died. She explained that her mother had worked cleaning a rich person's house to provide money, as her father was too weak to work. The hard work combined with the lack of food and the worry of her father's illness had made her mother ill, and in an attempt to try and make her daughter's eleventh birthday special she had stolen the purple hat from her employer's home. The hat, which had been a present for her employer's daughter, had been very expensive. It was made from the finest velvet and the feathers around the brim had been real ostrich.

The girl explained that when her mother handed her the colourful hatbox on her birthday and said that the present was from her and her father she was almost too afraid to open it. The box itself was a present on its own, with colourful stripes, fancy writing and tied with pink satin ribbon, but the contents were far beyond anything she could have imagined. She had carefully lifted the hat out of the box, feeling the soft velvet between her little fingers. The pink silk lining complemented the purple velvet perfectly, and the feather trim took her breath away. She placed the hat on her head and filled with excitement she danced around the room. Her father seated at the fire lifted his head and managed to smile, his eyes moist as he looked at his daughter. He felt so proud. It was to be her last birthday with both her parents and her mother made sure it would be one to remember.

The happiness was short lived as the police came to the house the following day. Her mother looking confused had been taken away, and her father was placed in hospital. Emily had been placed in an orphanage. She never saw her parents again.

"Becky, time to get up." Becky's mother came into the room. "Look at you asleep with Grandma Emily's hat still on your head, she's had that hat since she was eleven years old so you look after it."

Becky took the hat smoothed out the creases and placed it on her dressing table. It still looked beautiful she thought.

© Copyright Clarissa Kelly 2004

Council Tax Made Simple   Edwin Webster

The wise aul man, dumfoundert,
Speirt at the local feel,
"Fit's 'is cooncil tax aboot?
I wis nivir tellt in squeel."

The feel wis fulla learnin,
Wi twa or three degrees,
The wecht o knowledge in his heid
Gar him bowdy at the knees.

"The rich pay less, the peer pay mair.
It's ca'd equality.
Bit fan y stan up an object,
At's ca'd frivolity."

"Aul mannie, dinna fash yersel.
Dowp doon. Y'll bla a fuse.
The tax will catch y seen eneuch,
Awa hame furra snooze."

The aul boy pondered, then upspak,
"I mecht hae dam weel kint.
This cooncil is recht grippy, min.
Kin they cherge me furra tent?"

© Copyright Edwin Webster 2004

Whigmaleeries: A Word in Your Lug

The Performance   anne flann

She flung her strong, lithe body at him, and gave an inward smile at the small grunt the unexpected onslaught produced as her partner steadied himself against the impact. He bore her aloft in a high lift despite the shock at her ferocity.

"I'll give him 'ageing ballerina,'" she thought, having caught his muttered aside to a colleague in the wings during rehearsal. "The arrogance of this upstart – I'll show him what ballet really is," and she turned dark, reproachful eyes to gaze coldly, challengingly into his puzzled face as they continued their pas de deux.

Boris, the young dancer realised now that his chance remark had been overheard. At rehearsal week Tamara had constantly chided him about fumbled lifts, unsynchronised steps – anything and everything he did she had faulted. It was an undoubted honour to be selected to dance with this legendary prima ballerina but he was finding it a taxing experience, hence the careless comment to his friend as they waited offstage.

Alert now to her mood, he drew all his not inconsiderable talent to meet her flung down glove. His steps became more precise, his leaps higher, crisp and controlled. He danced as he had never danced before. And as each took stage in their alternating solos of intricate choreography, the audience sensed a new atmosphere, as did the corps de ballet joining them. A charged tension, an audacity permeated the stage – the audience edged expectantly forward in their seats and watched enthralled.

At interval, backstage was a-buzz with excitement. Through the chaos of costume change, powdered sweat, lacing pumps, whispered speculation couldn't ascertain why their principal dancers were virtually fighting an artistic dual in this already dramatic ballet – one new to their repertoire. In the men's changing rooms there was much raised eye contact, but Boris's friend kept his own counsel – he'd been fanning Boris's anger out of spite, annoyed that the younger man had been chosen as principal. In the star's dressing room the maitre de ballet tried to discover what was going on, to no avail. Boris merely shrugged and turned an uncommunicative back, while his dresser fussed irritatingly with his costume.

In the Circle bar the chatter was loud and excited. An elderly pair of balletomanes exchanged views. "Wasn't that a little, em, erotic? Why it was almost, well I don't like to say it Janet, but almost, well...." The wispy woman trailed off, peering diffidently over her specs. Her companion shook her head exasperatedly, "Really Mabel, sexy is the word, though why you should hesitate to use it, I don't know, what with all the fumblings, leg waving and lusty moans on telly these days! This is a memorable performance, I can't wait to get back to my seat." Mabel looked suitably chastened over her sherry and nodded humble assent. The warning bell sounded and there was a rush to return to seats, few lingered. A frisson of excitement trembled as the orchestra played the opening bars and the curtains rose. The quiver of violins and subdued drum roll brought the tension to almost unbearable pitch as the dramatic music of Bizet heralded the final act.

The company danced as they'd never danced before. Here was perfection and they responded to it with all the talent and training at their command. Tamara played her role with seductive fire and sensuality. Boris, virile and young, could not but respond to her tempestuous performance. She seduced him with her exotic, wanton interpretation and he felt the earthy attraction of the woman. Her beauty was timeless and she knew it. He had adulated her before she started her derogatory campaign. She had compared him unfavourably to her late partner with whom she'd had a fiery relationship for years. She resented one so young given such an opportunity when her Ivan had been taken so cruelly. Despite this she'd sensed the potential, admired Boris's dark, good looks. His nervous mistakes she knew full well were caused by her arrogant behaviour to him, and she'd loved the sense of power this gave her.

As she danced the final pas de deux with him she was stunned at his technique, his strength. She knew in the outside world she wasn't old, but in their rarefied world her 'shelf life' was dwindling – only a few like Pavlova, Fonteyne and Markova reigned supreme into their forties and fifties. She could emulate that with a new, vibrant partner. Tonight Boris was magnificent, they'd danced as one. She knew he was even better than Ivan had been. Now she wooed him with her dancing, pressing her body against him, feeling his excitement as they danced.

As they took the final curtain and bouquets were presented to the principals, the orchestra leader and the Maitre, she turned impulsively and handed Boris a rose and kissed his cheek. Turning to the audience she smiled that radiant irresistible smile for which she was noted – and gracefully indicated the young man with upturned hand in sheer acclaim – and the audience loved it. They left stage to clamorous applause, but did not return – she knew just when to strategically leave them wanting more.

The crits in the papers next day were deservedly complimentary. "A new partnership is born." "Boris Alessandro matches Fyodorovna's virtuosity and fire in a splendid new production." "An exciting event in the ballet world made enthralling theatre." In a café a bunch of Boris's fellow artistes from the ballet world, reading the notices remarked "Always had the luck of the devil, he did." One commented to his girlfriend, "Boris Alessandro indeed – he took the name Boris from a billboard and adapted his own name to Alessandro – sounds better than Jimmy Alexander! Still, he really is good, be as famous as Nureyev I shouldn't wonder." And so it proved.

Boris went from strength to strength, soon as famous in his own right as Tamara. As his virtuosity increased, often applause after his solos was even greater than Tamara's. They were the darlings of the ballet world, but as the years passed her age began to show. The

Whigmaleeries: A Word in Your Lug

strain of practice and performance taxed her more and more. He covered for her occasional inadequacies. A new Maitre de Ballet was appointed, younger, more modern and the repertoire extended to embrace more modern works. While Boris adapted to this with ease, Tamara did not. The Maitre decided Boris really needed a new partner. This was accomplished by replacing Tamara in modern ballets, pointing out that she did not enjoy them, while pairing her in such classics as Swan Lake and Fille Mal Gardee. Came the day when Tamara gracefully decided to retire. They gave a stunning final performance as partners to an emotional house of devotees.

A vivacious young ballerina now partnered Boris. It was while watching a rehearsal from the wings that Boris chanced to catch his young partner's whispered remark to another young dancer. "Isn't that Antoine terrific? I think Boris is getting past it – he can't be very young." "Here's where I came in." Thought Boris remembering.

© Copyright Anne Flann 2004

A Gey Aul' Desert Sang   Edwin Webster

Sandy hid bin an ill-trickit loon, wi his practical jokes an daftness. If, at the richt time, he hid bin geen a skelp roon the lug by his ma, a kick up the erse by his da, a good shakkin by the local bobby, an a dose o the scud fae the heidie, he micht hae turned oot a bittie better. But it didna happen an he became mair an mair o a damn nuisance. Even his ain mither came t' dislike him - "an evil little bugger" she ca'd him. There came a time, an there wis nae doot aboot it, fan he wis gan t be locked up, an for a lang time. A warrant for his arrest wis issued so Sandy decided t dee a runner. His ma gave him enough money t leave the country, in the sincere hope that he wid never return.

So Sandy wound up in France and jined the Foreign Legion. He'd read a book aboot the Legion. Weel, nae a book, nae really. Mair wan o them comic books wi picters an a sentence or so unnerneath. So he hid a romantic notion aboot the Legion. Saw himsel as a hero o the desert, in a funcy uniform, killin hunners o brown-skinned baddies an earnin dizzens o medals in the process. He wis soon disabused o that wee dream. Discipline wis harsh an Sandy hid nivir liked been telt fit t dee. Bullying in the Legion wis worse than in ony o the schools he'd bin kicket oot o in Aiberdeen. Now he wis the bullied, nae the bully. So he did fit he'd done afore – blamed abody else an run awa. Teen aff intae the desert.

But, now, lost in the desert, he wis feelin right sorry for himsel. He'd hae geen onything t' be back in Aiberdeen, even on a caul, weet day, stannin drookit in the Castlegate, wi the rain runnin doon his phizzog. Or spewin up his guts on a pub crawl doon Win'mill Brae. But here he wis, lost in the middle o the Sahara an nae signs o life, nae even an Arab onna camel.

He lurched onwards into a sea of sand, the dunes rising and falling in front of him like waves. The heat was unbearable and his throat was as dry as dust. His water was long gone. If he didn't get a drink soon, he would die of thirst. All he could do was stagger on and hope.

Were his eyes playing tricks on him? On the horizon there appeared a tiny speck, no bigger than a dot. He ploughed on through the cloying sand, blinking furiously. Had he seen a mirage? He peered again. The speck had grown larger. On and on he dragged his weary carcase, his body screaming for water, mouth as dry as a bone, and tongue like leather. The dot grew bigger and bigger until Sandy was able to discern a fellow human being, in a decaying physical condition, very similar to his own, staggering, ragged, obviously dehydrated. The two began to draw alongside, about fifty metres apart. Sandy thought, in horror: "My God! He's jist gan t walk on wi'oot a word." So he gathered himself together, tried desperately to clear his throat and rasped hoarsely and as loudly as possible: "HEY MIN!" The distant scarecrow stopped dead in his tracks, looked all around very slowly and deliberately, pointed theatrically to himself, opened his mouth and croaked: "FA? ME?"

Whigmaleeries: A Word in Your Lug

Haein' tellt sic a tired aul' tale, tak yur pick o three possible endings:

Sandy rescued by Good Samaritans. Transformed into the Sheikh of Araby.

Makes his way back to Scotland and becomes a model citizen, full of good deeds, a life devoted to charitable causes.

Captured and returned to the Legion. Locked up for desertion. Given a good kicking. Regularly.

Author's choice: No.3
Reason: The leopard disna change his spots; Sandy wis a right wee radge an' a good hidin wis lang owerdue!

© Copyright Edwin Webster 2004

The Train Journey   Sylvia Chesser

There was nothing exceptional about Bessie who was born under Cancer. In fact even her mother couldn't find anything that was remarkable, or especially worthy of note. Nobody ever really bothered about Bessie Bluebottle and it could honestly be said that she bothered nobody. Only one thing fascinated Bessie and that was the trains, which passed many times a day and most stopped at Stonehaven station.

Bessie did much the same thing every day and kept wondering what she could do that would be different from the usual routine. While resting at the picnic table, near Stonehaven Swimming Pool she heard a couple talking about their grandchildren who were having a gap year. They were visiting all sorts of strange sounding places and had been bungee jumping, paragliding and scuba diving. The women sounded as if they were proud, envious and anxious about their grandchildren's exploits.

"I think we should have one of these gap years, Sheila. Now that we are retired we could easily go off. Maybe we should forget about the extreme sports but we could have a lot of fun."

They seemed a really, happy pair as they went off chuckling to themselves. Bessie hoped they would go. Their conversation got her thinking again about her adventure. What should she do? She had done enough thinking it was time to spread her wings. She would go tomorrow.

Early next morning, Bessie decided to have the adventure and silently flew on to the train, just as the guard was signalling the driver. Near the door sitting at a table was a very respectable looking man in a suit, who was obviously trying to prepare for a meeting and was diligently reading and writing notes simultaneously. He was making appropriate responsive noises to the women opposite who was rapidly recounting her escapades in the supermarket. It would have been clear to everyone else but the storyteller that he was not interested or even listening. The poor women did not realise that a man cannot do three things at once! The man gave a slight sigh when he heard she was going to Edinburgh. He was hoping she was bound for Montrose.

The ticket collector came along and said "Any tickets from Stonehaven?" Luckily, Bessie being a nobody and insignificant was unseen and he carried on with his cry. "Any tickets from Stonehaven?" He proceeded, patiently plodding along. The train passed Montrose, Dundee and several other stations before reaching Perth. At Perth, the man put his papers, pen and paper away and banged his case shut. His head was whirring and he could concentrate no longer with the continual incessant chatter in his ear. He thought his wife could talk, but she was quiet compared to his travelling companion. It would have been better if he had not taken the earlier train to avoid travelling down with his colleague who told unfunny jokes and kept laughing at them. The same tired jokes would have been better than this chatter. He pretended to go to sleep. Surely she would stop now, but no, on and on the soliloquy went.

At last the train pulled in to Waverley, the man, the woman and Bessie got off. Bessie wondered where she would go? But whatever happened now, nobody could say she had never had an adventure. After all, it isn't every day that a bluebottle travels to Edinburgh on a train!

© Copyright Sylvia Chesser 2004

Twa Half-Croons   Edwin Webster

Auntie Aggie was a "character", described sometimes as "an affa wifie." She was a roly-poly little woman, cheerful and friendly, who gave the impression of having been born middle-aged. In fact, she had been born Agnes Jessie in Castle Street, Aberdeen in 1897, the year of Queen Victoria's Diamond Jubilee. Twice married, twice widowed, and twice a mother, Aggie led a strenuous life. When her mother's health began to deteriorate, she returned to an over-crowded tenement to keep house for her parents, brother, sisters, and her own children. She had a rich fund of tales to tell. I wish that I had paid more attention as a youngster, for I can recall only a few.

Aggie had a "good ear", and was a dab hand at "tickling the ivories", as piano playing was once known. I don't know if she had any formal music training but I doubt it. I never saw her play from music. She had, however, a natural talent and could churn out a recognisable version of any popular tune, having heard it only once or twice. She also had a wide repertoire of old Scottish favourites.

Because of her musical ability, she was much sought after at parties and all forms of social gatherings where a piano was available. Her popularity was at a premium during the Festive Season, especially Hogmanay. Many a reveller danced to Aggie's tunes. Word of her talents spread abroad and a local impresario acquired her services as a pianist at various functions organised by himself, such as weddings, anniversaries, birthdays and the like. Those were the days, in the 1920s and 1930s, when a solo pianist would provide an entire evening of music for a company, mostly for dancing. There were no pop groups for hire in those days, although a wealthy person, or "toff", might obtain the services of a light orchestra, or a dance band. Ordinary folk ended up with somebody like Auntie Aggie, were very grateful for it, and had just as good a time as your wealthy "nobs".

One "do", as a function was known, that Aggie played at, was for a farmer whose daughter had just been married. The "knees-up" took place in a hotel in Market Street. Aggie pounded the keys all evening as the teuchters whirled, twirled, skirled, birled, jigged, jagged, reeled, rolled and fell over. A great time was had by one and all.

At the end of the night, Aggie was paid £1 by her employer for her services. A couple of weeks later, she bumped into the fairmer who had footed the bill for his daughter's nuptials. He was effusive in his praise of her musical efforts and asked: "Did y' get the twa half-croons (25p) I gave the mannie for you?" Well, she never saw the five shillings in question, and her employer never mentioned the matter. It came as no great surprise that, in time, he and other members of his family became wealthy, and played a major role in entertainment in the city. He didn't just salt away his own pennies; he squirreled away other people's as well. Every time the family acquired another entertainment venue and it was announced in the local newspaper, Aggie would grimace, screw her eyes into slits, nod knowingly several times, and declare fiercely: "Weel, we a' ken far his siller came fae! Grumph!"

© Copyright Edwin Webster 2004

A Bourach...

The Cages anne flann

At one time in schoolrooms, children gathered round cages, their bright faces looming enormous to the tiny hamsters within. In one such cage, pausing now and then to raise twitching nose, then churning on his endless journey to nowhere on tiny pink feet was 'little Hammy'. "Isn't he cute?" "Just look, isn't he sweet?" cried the children. Pumping away on his fruitless travels, heart thumping to match frantic feet, little Hammy Hamster peered out through the bars – he hated their guts.

In the senior section of the old school, Mr Robertson paced irritably, slapping a book on his thigh as he tore a strip off Bennie Richmond. This was virtually a daily occurrence, for Benny was not the brightest pupil, but certainly the most disruptive. Each day the battle commenced, an unending feud of wills which left them both jangling and exhausted by the day's end. Bennie couldn't wait for the day he would leave school, Mr Robertson dreamt of retirement – but for now they too were trapped in their daily ritual.

At the zoo the lordly tiger yawned in boredom, stretching limbs, flexing claws. His great eyes surveyed the row of people and his eyes slitted. "There's a fine fat one" his mind registered, and licked his lips, long teeth gleaming as he again yawned. "One day, one day", was his hope. He rose to pace along the confining bars, and his mind flashed back to lush green grasses and a squealing pig.

Bepo the monkey sat picking through his fur, jabbering as his eyes flicked round looking for mischief to perform. He spied two elderly women watching him. One had an ancient silver fox cape, complete with dangling tails round skinny shoulders. "What a repulsive creature," she remarked to her companion, pointing to Bepo, who came close, staring fixedly. "Don't stand so near, Mabel," twittered her friend nervously – too late! Bepo's hand reached out, clasped the dangling fur and snatched the stole through the bars. He promptly skinned up to a high perch and sat idly picking through the fur, while the woman screeched her rage. Tearing the stole to shreds, he flung it down, and turned his back in disdain. "Silly old bitch – didn't even have fleas!"

The polar bear in his deep pit stood erect, head thrust forward peering at the murky water. His white coat dulled, yellowed, unlike the gleaming white of his relatives in the Arctic. He swings head from side to side, rocking powerful neck in anguished boredom before belly flopping into the stagnant pool. Not an ice flow in sight, no chance to roll in playful abandon in crisp deep snow, to stalk seal or penguin to satisfy hunger – or just for the joy of it.

Whigmaleeries: A Word in Your Lug

In the elephant enclosure great beasts shuffle feet and swing dry trunks in repetitive rhythm as though building restless energy to storm the confines. Their tactile trunks ever seek the pleasure of ripping down foliage with a satisfactory wrench, instead of lamely picking the fodder provided. Their small eyes weep into grey wrinkles and they idly blow dust over backs, longing for the relieving spray their keepers provide through hoses. "Oh to wallow in muddy waters in blissful freedom." They have long memories.

Old Jeanie Watson sits slumped before the lion enclosure, watching the elderly lion pace back and forth. His coat is patchy, mane sparse, bedraggled, but the golden eyes seem restlessly alert. "Poor old sod," Jeanie thinks, "not much better than me! Chained I am to that grouchy old bastard and his eternal benders. Expects me there at his beck and call. Chop him up, I should, and feed him to the bloomin' lion." She gives a gruff chortle at the idea, tickled pink, but she'll be there, serving up his steak and kidney, dancing attendance in the loveless monotony of a marriage made solely to get away from an equally demanding widowed father – escaping one tyranny for another.

Ah! That elusive freedom, those moments when one's spirit soars and the world seems boundless, horizons unlimited. We build our own cages, and live within.

Frances watches her children racing ahead while the youngest tugs impatiently at her hand. "Me too, me too," he cries, longing to run with his sisters. This mum enjoys her life, her children. She happily views their enthusiasm for these animals, glad that they are being preserved in a world rapidly losing vast numbers of species daily. Life for her seems great in her contentment, but others at desks, at kitchen sinks, classrooms, factories fret at the confines of their lives.

In an elegant office high above London a business tycoon sits toying with gold pen at his desk. "Just a couple more deals, then I'll retire." He rubs his left arm, massages his chest where of late pains niggle disquietingly. His doctor had shaken head and advised caution. "Not ready yet to hand over the reins. Young Andrew's hardly ready to take over though he thinks he is, young pup!" Andrew his son is a competent, hardheaded businessman with great entrepreneurial skill. He is nearly forty, but unlike his father enjoys his leisure. The father is chained to his desk by pride and the stubborn belief that he is indispensable.

And at the zoo gates, old Alfie sits behind the ticket machine as he has done for many years, resignedly taking in money, handing out tickets. "Two and an 'arf, sir? That'll be £10.85." He muses, "Day after day it's the same bloody grind, churning out tickets." He longs for the end of his day, his pinta, telly – and the old missus nagging away. "Hate to be cooped up like them poor beasts – what a life!"

© Copyright Anne Flann 2004

Be it Ever So Humble   Edwin Webster

In the summer of 1947, Auntie Aggie fae Aiberdeen went on holiday to Dundee. She had been invited to stay with friends, but as they were at work during the day, she had to amuse herself as best she could. Now, it may be merely a matter of opinion, but Dundee has never been the most interesting city in the world; not quite Paris, or Rome, or New York, for that matter. One day, at a loose end, Aggie decided to go on a Mystery Tour with a local bus company at a cost of seven shillings and sixpence (7/6d = 37p). It was a warm, sunny day, pleasant and relaxing, and Aggie slipped into a comfortable seat next to the window. The driver gave a running commentary as the trip began, and Aggie felt herself slip into a doze. She came to once or twice, with a start, but the driver's hypnotic drawl pulled her down into a deep sleep. She was well in the land of nod when the bus pulled to a halt. Slowly, she regained consciousness and looked out of the window. She could hardly believe her bleary eyes. They were in Castle Street, Aberdeen! The driver announced:

"And here we are, folks! Aberdeen! The Silver City with the Golden Sands. The beach and all its attractions lie to your right, the city centre and the shops to your left. Remember what they say about Aberdonians being tight? Make sure you count your change twice! You've got two hours to enjoy yourselves before we head back. OK? Well, have a good time. See you later."

Aggie stretched, sighed and got to her feet. Five minutes later, she was back home putting the kettle on and wondering how to kill the time until she was due to take the bus back to Dundee.

© Copyright Edwin Webster 2004

The Waitress

anne flann

Behind that round, enigmatic face, that stolid-seeming countenance lurks a rapier mind. Maggie herself doesn't even realise it, sunk in her niche of lower class acceptance of her place in the world.

She sidles round the tables with her damp cloth and spray cleaner wiping endlessly, absorbed totally in her task. Maggie takes pride in the spotless sheen of her tables and tuts irritably when confronted by cigarette ash, crumbs and blobs of sauce, shaking her head ruefully, causing the strained back pony tail to bounce, releasing straggling ends to curl on her neck and frame her face.

A sigh escapes as a plump fortyish woman drops into her newly cleaned table by the window. "Shit – hoped that good looking bloke would get there first, just my luck!" She glowers dourly as the cute blonde waitress, who doesn't give a damn about cleaning tables – but never mixes up orders, leans seductively over the male customer, smiling warmly while pointing out items on the menu and incidentally revealing a modest cleavage.

Maggie does sometimes get orders wrong, her mind on other things, like the ring on her customer's finger. "Cor, must have cost a fortune that, big as a marble. Nah! Must be fake, one of them zirconiums or something. Cheap as they come she is – bit past it, music hall type. Look at them roots, need touching. Still, the fur coat's real, mink – wonder she's got the nerve to wear it these days with all them Animal Rights crowd – maybe she feels she earned it!" Maggie chuckles at the thought, while nodding and affirming that, 'Yes the salads are very nice' and taking the order for a Caesar salad, with barbequed chicken.

"Chicken Caesar," she bawls to the chef and scurries back as one of her favourite customers enters and is about to take one of the blonde's tables. "This one here's cleared, sir." She sings out in a surprisingly musical voice – and smiles broadly as the young waitress in turn glowers at her. This customer is a tipper of some magnitude – Maggie ain't stupid!

And so it goes – clear and serve, clear and serve, while all the time Maggie's brain goes clickety-click, summing up the folk with amazing accuracy. Two women, mother and daughter enter with a small girl. "Nouveau riche", thinks Maggie, hugging the phrase to her proudly. They sit at the head waitress's table and Maggie breathes a sigh of relief, viewing the three petulant faces.

Divesting themselves of expensive coats they order wine and "I want coke", whines the child loudly, "Don't want milk." There's much discussion over the menu and a loud "But I WANT it," seems to settle the matter as mother shrugs. Drinks are placed. The blonde mother, lovely but with a downturn to mouth which spoils the effect, sips her wine, grimacing at the quality.

Grandmother looks regal and shrugs shoulders in cashmere sweater, turning to reprimand the child's persistent interruption of conversation. The food is brought and little madam screws up her face. "I don't like it," and pushes the untouched plate away. Mother's lips compress, "You asked for it darling, you'll damned well eat it." Wails are stifled as the two women stare her down and she subsides into snifflles. The mother beckons Maggie imperiously. No sign of their own waitress, so Maggie obliges. "Take that away, please," mother waves imperious hand in the direction of the child's food. "Shall I bring something else?" asks Maggie as great tears roll down 'darling's' face. "No, she'll just do without," mother states coldly, whereupon the child grabs back her plate and proceeds to gobble it down.

Maggie shrugs resignedly and returns to her own tables where a middle-aged gentleman now sits scanning the menu. "Nice old bloke," she considers and smiles, warming her face into a kind of beauty, not noticeable in repose. He peers up at her through gold-rimmed specs, his refined face quizzical. "What would you recommend today?" "Well, the soup's specially nice, warming on a cold day and good value if you select a filled roll – or the stews specially good." He nods, "Yes, I'll have the soup and roll, please." "The ham's home cooked, nice and lean," she suggests helpfully and the man nods assent with a pleased smile.

The place fills, all four waitresses are fully occupied with the rush. Plates are gathered, coffees dispensed, lunchtime nearly over. Maggie ruefully rubs her back and wipes clean the last table. In the midst of all the bustle she has hit the nail on the head assessing customers, their status and characters to a T.

Homeward bound she pauses before the careers shop, and pops in. There are often brochures of evening classes scattered around and she picks a few up. She'd left school early to ease the burden on elderly parents; but hankered after some 'learning'. Home she slips her feet gratefully into mules, pops on kettle and sinks into her worn old chair. She peruses the brochures and pauses over the write up about a psychology class. "Guess I haven't enough education for that," she sighs.

Go for it, Maggie – it's right up your street!

© Copyright Anne Flann 2004

Whigmaleeries: A Word in Your Lug

Greetings   Edwin Webster

The last time I'd been there, it had been a real old-fashioned workingman's bar; dark, dingy, fuggy with smoke, reeking of stale beer and full of ferret-faced wee mannies in bunnets, engaged in Scotland's national pastime – takkin a bucket. The refurbished premises were bright and shiny, the artificial lighting so intense that it hurt the eyes. The original bar and gantry, of Edwardian creation, had been torn out and replaced by a hardboard and vinyl structure.

I bought a pint and took a seat in a corner. It was approaching midday and the place was beginning to fill up with lunchtime customers. Suddenly, the door was flung open, and what I took to be a local yobbo waltzed in. However, when he took off his jacket and bounced behind the counter, I realised that he was a barman starting his shift. His dark hair was cut short and he was generally neat and tidy but, like most of his generation, he was a stranger to shoe-polish. The youthful clientele knew him well and the banter flowed. A few minutes into his shift and he made his selection from the jukebox. Pop music, played at reasonable level, I can tolerate, but this character (Baheid the barman, I christened him) turned the volume up full blast. Glasses and ashtrays rattled on tabletops, walls and floor vibrated, and the fillings in my teeth started to come loose. Death by Meatloaf.

Baheid wasn't finished. He bustled about, full of bumptiousness and bonhomie, collecting empties and dispensing his own brand of wit and wisdom. He stopped at my table and, above the deafening noise of the jukebox, bellowed:

"Cheer up, pal. It's nae the end o the world. This is a fun bar. Smile, min, smile!"

I bared my teeth in a grimace and replied: "It's not compulsory, is it?"

He blinked and moved on bombarding others with his personality, or lack of it. Young women in particular, took to him. He never gave up. Every time he passed my table, he exhorted me to "Cheer up." I didn't again rise to the bait. I tried to swallow my irritation, but it kept coming back, like heartburn.

The youngster didn't realise that a miserable exterior can often hide an inner contentment and also, that it's the right of every individual to remain aloof from the horde, if he wishes. I was just thinking about leaving when Baheid went on his next round of showing off. He collected over twenty pint tumblers and was carrying them in a single stack in his cupped hands. A waitress followed in his wake, carrying a tray laden with the remains of bar lunches. Baheid was so intent on astounding his audience that he didn't see what I had seen – a patch of grease on the floor where someone had spilt gravy from a pie. I held my breath as Baheid pranced on. Sure enough, he stepped right on the greasy spot and his feet flew from under him. As he fell backwards, the stack of glasses shot into the air, divided, and shattered on the floor all around the stricken barman. As he fell, he banged into the waitress, who staggered sideways, shrieked, and dropped her heavy-laden tray. Plates and scraps of food flew in all directions.

Broken glass lay everywhere but, fortunately, no-one was injured. Baheid lay, shaken and stirred, but unhurt. A thin strip of lettuce was plastered across his forehead, a slice of tomato lay on his Adam's apple, a piece of onion dangled off the tip of his nose, and the remains of a pie and chips was strewn across his shirt-front.

As I stood up and prepared to leave, I looked down on the fallen warrior, lying amidst the debris, and injecting as much venom as I could muster into my voice, hissed the dreaded words:

"Have a nice day."

© Copyright Edwin Webster 2004

A New Leaf   Sylvia Chesser

Mr. MacHaggis was leaning on the rake in his garden. His garden was immaculate. No sooner had a weed dared to peep through and he removed it. It wasn't a big garden but it always had a lot of colour, which cheered everyone on his or her way to the shop or the bus. It was strange that Mr. MacHaggis had the opposite effect on everyone. Nobody could describe him as cheerful. Even his friends, if he had any, would have to say he was a moaner. People stopped to admire his garden and they chuckled at the large gnome, which stood in the corner and had a huge grin on its face. However, if mistakenly they said something with even a vaguely happy tone, Mr MacHaggis always either just grunted or gave them a very pessimistic reply. His favourite topic was about how young people today were hopeless, messy and lazy. Not like in his day when National Service smartened them up. Not, of course, that he needed smarting, his days in the Boys Brigade had seen to that.

Today it was the paperboy that he was complaining about. He had wakened him up at seven o'clock whistling as he came up the path. What had he to whistle about? Yesterday, he had seen the same lad carrying Mrs. Brown's shopping. Cheerily talking as he kept pace with her slow walk, obviously, hoping she would give him a tip. Nobody carried his shopping. He was organised and he ordered all his bulky items, which were delivered.

Then there was that teenager yesterday asking if he would like to buy a ticket to a Ceilidh they were having at the Community Centre. What would he want to go to a Ceilidh for? She said it was to raise funds for a new Hospice for Children. He'd read in the paper about these bogus schemes before. It said they often were just raising money for themselves. Even if it was for a Hospice, the Ceilidh's noise would probably be so loud that he'd hear it when he was trying to listen to the radio or sleep.

He remembered Marigold, who lived across the street, but was meantime off on her gap year, working in South America with street children. She could have stayed here and helped with the old people in her own street, instead of gadding off half way across the world.

Oh dear! Here was Mrs. MacCheery or whatever her name was, grandmother of the ever-happy paperboy. She was always jolly and tried to make light conversation with him. He knew all about all her various exploits, volunteer at the hospital, reading on to audio tapes for the blind, doing bits of shopping for anyone who was ill, looking after her grandchildren and she still always had time to chat to people.

"Hallo. How are you today?" Asked Mrs. MacCheery.

Should he tell her that he was miserable because his wife had died ten years ago today? His memory was going and he felt he had the early signs of dementia. He couldn't sleep at night because he was worried that he couldn't pay all his bills and he wasn't going to go cap in hand to the State. She didn't know his only son had been killed in action at 19. He did love his garden though and perhaps he should turn over a new leaf and try harder to make friends and stop thinking so much about himself. Here goes. "That's a fine grandson you've got, always helping people."

© Copyright Sylvia Chesser 2004

Whigmaleeries: A Word in Your Lug

Travelling Companions   anne flann

The journey to Edinburgh that day seemed interminable. Normally it was a journey that I savoured, that early morning ride to the Capital. I always sat on the left facing the engine so as to see all the favourite coves between Aberdeen and Stonehaven. The wooded area where a stream meandered – there one could spot roe deer drinking in the early morning light. Once I'd spied a doe and her fawn. The doe had drunk unperturbed but the fawn raised a started head as the train chugged by. It was on this line too that I'd spotted my first badger, snuffling his way up the embankment when the train slowed for a signal. I loved the sea views, and had bays that I longed to explore – and never did. Settling back in my seat I turned my attention to the man opposite.

A slender, scholarly face topped with greying hair gazed thoughtfully out of the window while slim fingers tapped a rhythm on the table between us. At Stonehaven a small group entered the carriage, and a stout, elderly woman plunked herself down on the seat beside me. She was laden with an assortment of bags and packages; a battered case, two plastic bags bulging at the seams, and besides an enormous unwieldy handbag, a vast knitting bag dangled from her arm. He rose and helped her settle her case and ruefully eyed the clutter which she proceeded to strew on the table; a People's Friend, daily paper, tattie crisps, a bag containing two morning rolls and a battered thermos flask, which she shortly unscrewed, wheezing, "Didn't have time for breakfast, so I brought it with me." She grinned a cheery smile and poured herself a redolent cup of coffee.

Our companion settled back opposite and after the first disbelieving stare, flicked open his newspaper, which he scanned with increasing boredom, shaking his head at some article which met with disapproval, or nodding in silent agreement with some comment. This held his attention for some time between occasional glances at passing scenery. A contained sort of restlessness caused him to fidget in his seat, and long legs obviously rendered the journey less than comfortable. He whipped out a pen and proceeded to do the crossword, which took him little time at all. He closed the paper with crisp efficiency, either annoyed at the simplicity of the puzzle, or satisfied at his own acumen. The fingers continued their drumming as he gazed out of the window, deep in thought.

All this time the stout woman kept up a running conversation with me, between large bites of her 'rowie' and gulps of coffee. It appeared she was visiting her sister in Edinburgh – and my heart sank in the knowledge that she'd be going all the way too. After learning of her sister's unhappy marriage, her own Charlie's problems with his boss, and her daughter's unwanted pregnancy, I was about at screaming point. I glanced up and caught the flicker of amusement in the eyes opposite. He gave a twisted little smile, one-sided and wry, and folding his arms closed those intelligent grey eyes – and I followed suit as the only way to stem the flow. On awakening, I noticed she had immersed herself in the People's Friend, and breathed a sigh of relief. I met those grey eyes across the table and smiled. He returned it briefly, but his thoughts were obviously far away. From time to time he rumpled the tight crisp curls of his hair, or tugged the lobe of his ear, as though in deep thought. While the plump soul beside me, drowsing now, snored with a peculiar but soft flutter, he unbended enough to point out a seal perched on a rock, scratching contentedly at chest with fins. We exchanged reminiscences of happenings on past journeys but he was obviously distracted, mind on other things than the flora and fauna of Scotland.

The journey drew to a close – the last few miles seeming the longest before drawing in to Waverley Station. He assisted the old dear down with her bulging case, where she stood, surrounded by her plastic bags greeting a thin, gaunt-faced woman who vaguely resembled her; then handed me down from the train and I took his arm. Before we could speak we spotted the grinning face of our son-in-law Brian greeting us beyond the barrier. He looked tousled and flushed with excitement. "It's a boy," he yelled as we approached, and my husband's face broke into the first real smile in days. "Jan's just fine, no trouble at all – they were delighted with her – 8lbs 6oz he was" – the words tumbled out and he scooped me in a bear hug, while Don clapped him heartily on the back. I glanced at my husband's radiant face – gone was the austere, scholarly look, the withdrawn air which gave him a look of disdainful superiority. His face was as boyish and animated as Brian's – and I wondered if Jan too was ever amazed at the dual personality of her own college professor.

© Copyright Anne Flann 2004

Media Star

Edwin Webster

Fit an awesome thing t' be.
"A TV Personality."
"Chat Show Host." Min, fit a caker,
Deen up like an undertaker.
'Ey say it's teuch, bit 'at's a' lees,
A life o' parasitic ease.
Canna dunce, or act, or sing,
Nae dam eese at onything.
Jist sit 'ere, lookin' unco glaikit,
Weerin' some fantooshie jaikit.
Clarty smirk a' ower yur face,
'At fix't it maun be shewn i' place.
Teeth sae perfec' nivir grew,
Ten thoosan punsworth in yur mou'.
Yur ainly gifties, clack an blether
Wi' ither "stars", a' feels igither.
Bit mebbe y'r nae sic a gowk,
Yur siller comes fae us peer fowk.
"I'm tops", 'e TV conman gloats.
'At's true eneuch, for keech aye floats.

© Copyright Edwin Webster 2004

Family Album

anne flann

Photographs faded
stained with age
or torn and crumpled
in momentary rage
Depicting each scene
each moment from youth
to reflect passing moments
but seldom full truth

What the occasion?
Each frozen tooth smile
did they mask discontent
or sorrow
or joy smiling out?
Time capsules caught
for those that follow
here's what life's all about?

Nothing is ever
as black or as white
as those portraits,
moments recorded in time
Lightness and darkness
gaiety, sorrow
remembrances left
for those of tomorrow

Mere contrasting shadows
of what has been
captured moments of drama
from that swift passing scene

© Copyright Anne Flann 2004

Whigmaleeries: A Word in Your Lug

Ooyah! Ooyah! Ooyah!   Edwin Webster

Aggie and her pal decided to be very bold and go and watch the wrestling matches at the Music Hall. Although this was largely a male prerogative, the two had heard of a handful of wifies who attended, so they decided to have a shottie themselves. Wrestling was very popular in Aberdeen after the Second World War; bouts took place on a Tuesday evening at 7.30pm and were well attended. The contestants were primarily showmen who brought a touch of glamour into the grey drabness of a postwar city. They had fanciful nicknames, like "Butcher", "The Mauler", and "Bonecrusher". One performer claimed to be a full-blooded Red Indian and called himself "Chief Running Bull" or some such nonsense. He wore a feathered headdress and performed a war dance before each contestant. The headdress and war dance were probably as genuine as a £3 note and the nearest he had been to the Wild West was watching a John Wayne film. However, authentic or not, the audience lapped it up. Another grappler wore a black mask and the story went that he was hideously scarred, hence the disguise, but it was just another piece of theatrical patter.

The wrestlers adopted extreme roles. Some were goodies – whiter than white, supreme sportsmen who would never take unfair advantage of an opponent; on the other hand, there were the baddies – double-dyed villains, hate figures, who would stoop to the lowest possible depths to defeat a rival. Baddies were always much more interesting than goodies.

Wrestling had a language all of its own. Every move, every hold had a word or a phrase to describe it – Forearm Smash, Flying Mare, Double Nelson, Headlock, Bodyslam, Chokehold, Boston Crab. An evening's entertainment consisted of six "all-in" bouts. The wrestlers made their way down the aisles, clad in fancy, colourful dressing gowns, either booed or cheered, according to the individual's reputation. After clambering through the ropes, they went into the usual ritual of stripping off the dressing gowns, flexing their muscles, limbering up and generally playing to the crowd, before the referee called them to the centre and administered the standard warning: "Now, I want a good, clean contest. No biting, no spitting, no gouging, no punching."

A great deal of violence seemed to go on in the ring but no one was ever badly hurt, although once in a blue moon someone would be carted off on a stretcher. The wrestlers knew how to fall so as to avoid injury. When a contestant hit the canvas with a massive thump, it seemed impossible that he would ever get up again. But, nine times out of ten, bounce up again he did. A wrestler, who was being forced to submit, seemed to endure tortures and agony beyond belief; you wondered how anyone could withstand such pain! Spectators got caught up in the excitement of the occasion and applauded or jeered at the top of their voices. All the ingredients were there – the heady mixture of sweat and embrocation, the violence of the clash between two modern gladiators, the noise of the crowd – all these produced a chemistry that added to the thrill of the event.

When the evening came to an end, everything returned to normal and it became a question of getting outside and going home. Aggie and her friend, two eminently respectable, middle-aged wifies, complete with hats, had had a whale of a time. This would be something to tell their cronies in the chipper; their adventure watching the grunt-and-groan brigade. However, getting out of the Music Hall was a slow process. They bauchled along, shuffling up the aisle, hemmed in by a solid phalanx of men. Progress was snail-like. Their exhilaration had begun to fade and the tiredness of a long, hard day was creeping up on them. Their feet were sair. Shuffle, shuffle. Follow the crowd. Keep shuffling on and eventually you'll get outside. Would they never reach an exit? Then progress came to a virtual standstill and they noticed that those ahead of them were heading towards a long white-tiled wall. They were in the gents' toilet.

© Copyright Edwin Webster 2004

Whigmaleeries: A Word in Your Lug

The Stamp of Adventure
Written Christmas 2002

Sylvia Chesser

Do you crave for adventure? The anticipated excitement enveloping you in a warm glow. Then just as your imagination hits a crescendo you relax and recline further back into your comfy armchair, stealthily savouring all the varieties in a box of chocolates in an aura of calm contentment, whilst conjuring up images of exotic lands and daring deeds.

However, if you do venture off your chair, a mini adventure may be closer than you think and even a bit close for comfort. It can even cost very little. My one even saved me the cost of a first class stamp and gave me some much-needed exercise. Now that can't be bad! The card for my friend who lives in a multi-storey required posting. However, I decided to get off the bus a few stops earlier, walk there and deliver the card. Nothing difficult or sensational there. But hold on; don't nod off yet, as the drama is about to liven up.

The card was silently posted through my friend's letterbox and I tiptoed to the lift. Silly when I needed the exercise, but it turned out that I sweated much more than had I used the stairs. A young man, of about 20, was standing there. He was carrying a carved wooden sword. As we waited for the lift I remarked it was nicely carved. However, all was not what it seemed. It all too soon transpired that the wooden sword was actually just the case.

In the lift he immediately took out the sword and flourished it with a few fearsome swishes. It looked frighteningly fearsome and shiny. I clutched my handbag a bit tighter. My brain went into sharp spasms. Huge headlines high-jumped into my mind; **"Elderly lady gets slashed in skyscraper!"** Have you noticed that anybody over 50 is elderly in newspapers? **"Scottish pensioner fights off swordsman in skyscraper."** My mind was working at high-speed and the adrenaline was flowing fast. This wasn't the time to be a hero or heroine nor to have a senior moment! How could I get myself out of this situation and remain in one piece?

In the past, I had always talked myself out of scary situations. If I talked enough he might decide I was too boring to bother with.

"That's a great sword. Where did you get it?"

"On holiday in Turkey."

"How much did it cost?"

"I can't remember. Not sure why I bought it. I was very drunk at the time. I haven't used it yet."

The "yet" rattled me a bit. He obviously felt he hadn't got his money's worth yet. Better try some more chat to take his mind off the fact that he hadn't tried it yet. My mind raced. Why was he carrying a sword? A highland dancer would need two swords and he definitely didn't look like a sword swallower. Whatever he was going to do with it, I'd better continue the chat.

"Where are you going with it?"

"To the pawn shop. Don't know how much its worth though."

The lift seemed to be taking forever. Somebody said that these multi-storey lifts do sometimes suddenly stop in mid-air. Its funny how a few minutes can seem to stretch forever. At last we were there.

I certainly felt safer now we were on the ground floor. Someone would hear me screaming and I could try to run for it. My thoughts pleaded, just save me and I promise I'll get fitter and eat less chocolate.

After all my anxiety and angst what happened? He simply said, "Bye. Take care." He walked off swinging the sword, now in its case and no doubt dreaming of how much he would get for it in the pawn shop.

But an adventure is never wasted. When someone corners me and tells me how brave they were when they saw tigers, or risked their neck white water rafting, I'm ready with my tale. Not sure whether in Aberdeen they will be more impressed that I met a swordsman in a skyscraper, or that I saved the cost of a stamp.

© Copyright Sylvia Chesser 2004

Top Marks

An Affa Sair Belly   Edwin Webster

During the War (World War Two 1939-45, NOT the Crimean War), I was a hospital patient a number of times. It was never a pleasant experience. At that time, and in that place, a knowledge of child psychology was the last thing a nurse needed. On one occasion, when I was seven years old, I came home from school doubled up in pain. It was agonising. There was no local doctor in our area, only a district nurse. She was an aged crone, with a hatchet face and a sharp beak of a nose; she had iron-grey hair and matching complexion. She should have been retired but the needs of the war kept her in business. She went her rounds on an ancient bicycle, pedalling frantically along the highway, sometimes reaching a speed of three miles per hour, and even occasionally overtaking an elderly pedestrian.

She didn't know that I had an abscessed appendix, but she knew my condition was serious and duly summoned an ambulance. I was carried downstairs on a stretcher and put in the meat-wagon. I recall a kindly, avuncular ambulance man trying to reassure me. I'm sure he would have patted my head if his hands had not been fully occupied.

"You'll be all right, son", he said. "You won't feel a thing. Just like having a tooth out. You'll be right as rain. Back home in no time."

Lying old sod.

I spent three weeks in hospital and I did not enjoy it.

© Copyright Edwin Webster 2004

The Lone Seat

anne flann

She entered the hall, looking to neither side. Gliding as though on ice, her sari floating in soft waves around her in the slight breeze from the open door. She held a child by the hand, a small replica of herself, with the same enormous dark eyes, heavily lashed, and silken, ebony hair with a hint of blue. Silently she walked past all the waiting women, holding her head even higher. She reached the seat beyond the waiting crowd and sat, drawing the child to her with slim, brown arm, bangles jangling metallically, the only sound she made.

She was there every day without fail, exactly on time, and always that seat seemed available, as though the others left it deliberately for her, isolated, apart. Daily I watched her to see if any spoke, or if she herself approached any of the other mothers – but no. Each day she walked her queenly way past the throng to that lonely chair.

And out they'd tumble, hand in hand, jostling, laughing, pushing, shouting. Blonde, black and red-haired children in a veritable rainbow of clothes. And there, my own copper headed grandson, hand in hand with a diminutive Indian boy. They were grinning and chatting excitedly together. There was a joyous look of mischief and fun about the pair. The little boy spotted his mother, quietly withdrew his hand and solemnly walked to his mother's side. He grasped the hand of the tiny girl and the three walked sedately through the crowd, looking neither to left or right, till they disappeared from sight through the exit door.

Chandra had quaked the first time she entered the school with her small boy, clutching her tiny daughter's hand, while he strode off, stiff-backed before her. She was new to this town, though not Britain, and dreaded the necessity of starting all over again the process of trying to make friends with local women, fumbling her way through a maze of attitudes. Back home she had had prestige, daughter of a respected merchant. Here she was a no-one, wife of a student doctor who worked all hours, never at home with her and the children. She had no contact, no friends around. Now she was entering a different phase – her first born going to school. Would she be accepted? Pride had stiffened her straight back and she'd marched past them all to the waiting seat and sat aloof, head high, eyes lowered. She looked so unapproachable that none spoke, and so it had remained.

It was the children who broke the spell. One chatty little blonde child stood sucking her thumb before her. Pulling it out with a soft 'plop' she asked "Why are you so pretty – are you a Princess or a fairy queen? My Mummy always wears jeans – I like your dress." Her mother laughed, giving her a tiny shake of reproof and said to Chandra, "You DO look sort of royal. That sari is gorgeous, but I'd look pretty silly in that with my spiky hair." "No, no," protested Chandra, "It is I who look strange – my husband's not wanting me to wear European clothes, but I would like to."

Soon all the mothers in the vicinity were joining in excitedly. "You should please yourself what you wear," said one. "Tell him you're in Britain now," cried another. "You should jolly well please yourself, " insisted one feminist. The others laughed, knowing her attitude only too well. "But why would you wear anything else?" asked another "You look so wonderful – I wish I looked like that."

The animated babble died down gradually, and the little blonde girl took the Indian boy's hand and the two children ran off down the corridor, while the jean-clad mother and the graceful Indian followed, chatting quietly together, the tiny girl skipping between them, holding both hands.

The seat remained empty for the rest of that term – perhaps waiting the next shy foreigner, afraid to approach lest she offend. Isolated often merely by language barrier it is hard to make that first step. Yet deep down we are all the same, we mothers. The children are, in this, the teachers – they see only another child to play with, irrespective of race or colour. They communicate despite language, are enchanted by anything foreign, or different. They only acquire their prejudices as they grow up. They hold out their warm little hands and run together, play together, learn together, even squabble and fight together – and then they grow up.

© Copyright Anne Flann 2004

Whigmaleeries: A Word in Your Lug

Millicent

Clarissa Kelly

Millicent had been awake for some time. She could hear the muffled voices of her parents and the Radio Two presenter in the kitchen below. The smell of her father's bacon wafted up from downstairs.

"A good breakfast sets you up for the day", he would say to Millicent as she toyed with her cereal. She was not a morning person.

Just then her mother called. "Are you up Millicent? You'll be late for school." Weekdays, especially Mondays, were a low point for Millicent. Since she started 'big' school she had lost her two best friends who had gone to a different school, and had been unable to make new ones. She had tried very hard during her first year, maybe too hard she thought, as she was still friendless.

Millicent's parents were married a long time before she came along and as an only child she was very precious to them and they lavished their attention on her. She was encouraged to try everything from the Brownies to kick boxing, and she embraced them all with great enthusiasm. Her father had taught her to play chess and now she beat him regularly.

Millicent was tall and tidily dressed, some would say old-fashioned. She worked well in her classes and was liked by her teachers.

Being in a class filled with Chloes, Kirstys and Rachels, Millicent seemed a dull name and in the first days of school when her name had to be given in class she felt the odd one out. The other girls would snigger quietly, but loud enough for Millicent to hear.

Millicent asked her mother why she had chosen that name and she had said she was named after a singer from the 1960s. Lulu was from the same era thought Millicent, now that would have been a cool name.

Recently a clique of girls, the ones who wore make-up and high heels to school, had started being more daring towards Millicent. Several times in the corridor as they made their way to a different class, Millicent would find herself on the floor having been tripped up. This accidental 'bumping' into her had been happening more often as was the group whispering when she approached. Millicent was feeling very low and isolated but to tell her parents or teachers she thought would make matters worse.

Millicent's mother had noticed a change in her daughter, but thought the moping around the house and the long spells spent in her bedroom was just a part of growing up. She did not suspect that Millicent was being bullied. She did wonder why no friends from school came to the house or why Millicent never seemed to be invited to birthday parties like before, but she put these thoughts out of her head, convinced that if Millicent had a problem at school she would tell her.

The Annual School's Chess Championship loomed ahead and Millicent, who was a member of the school chess club, spent most of her free time perfecting her moves. This was the only time when she was happy at school.

The chess club was mixed and all the boys and girls got on well together. The best player was Jamie, he was also the best looking guy at school. He was tall and when skateboarding with his baggy trousers and gelled hair, all the girls hung around him, he was so cool. Jamie liked Millicent. She was not like the other girls who tried to get his attention. She was quiet but very interesting. She knew such a lot and she played a mean game of chess. She did look a bit old-fashioned but he thought she had a very pretty face and he had taken a liking to her.

As the chess competition between the schools progressed it was apparent that Millicent's school was well ahead and looked to be the likely winners. The final was Millicent and Jamie against a pair from another school. Millicent and Jamie played a stormer, securing the cup and prestige for their school in a flamboyant manner.

After the chess tournament Millicent and Jamie continued their friendship and spent lots of time together. Millicent noticed that the bumping into and the 'accidental' tripping up had stopped, likewise the whispering and the sniggering. Her female classmates were now eager to speak to her, especially when she was with Jamie. I wonder, she thought to herself, if this is because I was part of the winning chess team, or she smiled inwardly, because Jamie and I are now an item?

© Copyright Clarissa Kelly 2004

A Red Letter Day   George Crossan

It was the end of prize-giving; more specifically, the end of term. I was walking towards the staff room, taking off my gown as I went. I was to meet some colleagues in town for a celebratory end-of-term lunch. There were smiles on pupils' faces, some laughter, and some respectful greetings from parents.

A familiar sound pricked my ear for a moment. I dismissed it. There it was again slightly louder, more pronounced, "Mr Crawford". I stopped, hesitantly. In those surroundings, I wasn't used to hearing my name so politely defined. More common, was a 'Stuart' (from my colleagues) or a slightly grudging 'Sir', from students.

As I turned to look, I could see Kenneth Scott's red head above everybody else's. He was waving his arm as he called out my name, his hand grasping the prize for literature that he had earlier received in the Hall. He was a bit pink in the face, boyishly excited, breathless and attractively gauche as he reached me, stumbling over words. 'Sorry, sir … thanks, sir … wanted to catch you before you left … before I left … it was your fault … you did it … I couldn't have did it – done it, sir – before. Thank you. Thank you very much.' He stopped. He looked embarrassed now that we were closer together. There was no need to say more. We both understood.

'You did it all yourself, Kenneth', I said. 'No one else. I was just an old buffer your train ran into. You needed to change direction. And you did'. He half nodded, still smiling, in muted acknowledgement. I muttered a few more polite noises, shook hands with him, smiled and moved on. 'Thank you, sir', he shouted after me.

I was pleased. Teaching is a risky business. It's not like creating artefacts in a factory. There, you can see or can be told when your workmanship is bad. It's not so easy in teaching. By what rule are your efforts to be measured? Or by whom? How can you prove that you are not passing on damaged opinions? For that reason, when someone thanks you, it can seem like a red letter day.

I had met Kenneth barely a year before. The headmaster had asked me to take him into my class. 'You know Scott', he said. 'I know only of him', I reminded him, unhelpfully. 'He's had a bad time,' he added, not wishing to be thwarted. 'He's failed his Highers twice. You're pretty good with dumplings. See what you can do with this one'. I accepted the challenge, ungraciously, reminding the headmaster that Kenneth Scott's reputation suggested that it was not he who had had the bad time, but his teachers.

Scott was instructed to report to me right away. After three weeks, he had not appeared. He was being 'smart', or thought he was. He wasn't truanting. He was reporting to his registrar in the morning, and disappearing for the rest of the day. Hearsay suggested that he was spending a lot of time at the playing fields, excusing himself by claiming that he had been specially asked to help out in the PE Department. I sent for him.

He appeared the following day, early, before the others had assembled. He started to apologize. I told him to sit down: I would tell him when to speak. When the class was fully assembled, I asked him to stand up and to direct himself to his new classmates. It's doubtful if I felt any sympathy for him. He was just refusing to grow up.

"Tell them," I said, "why you've been avoiding them. It's not only me you have to convince of your seriousness. It's their time you have been wasting, by your shenanigans. They're being asked to change their year's study pattern to accommodate you. Don't you think they deserve an explanation? Even an apology?"

He stuttered and stammered, trying to excuse himself. The empty grin on his face had disappeared. When he would make an effort to sit down, I would unhelpfully ask him another question. Could he suggest possible reasons why he might have failed in the past: this would be his third attempt? I made it clear to his classmates, 'He's going to be wasting his time and ours', I observed, dryly, unless he changes his ways. 'Kenneth', I said, 'If you don't want to pass, go home. Get a job. Do something useful with your life.' He looked shocked.

I refused to let him sit down. I knew he was uncomfortable. I was being awkward. I encouraged the others to ask him questions, civilly, but seriously.

In the end, and with some relief on all sides, the whole affair developed into a class discussion on the subject itself, its difficulties, typical students' problems, and the place of the 'Highers' (if they were to have a place) in the future development of their careers. He sat down slowly, tentatively, a little more at peace with himself. Nobody complained.

Not one person had made any profound observation, or revealed any shattering truth about the nature of learning. But what had, perhaps, come across strongly was the extent to which the others cared. Maybe that was a new experience for Kenneth. Whatever the truth of it, he stayed.

Was I cruel? I don't know. Certainly one of my colleagues who heard about the session, thought so. That wasn't my aim. Probably, I could be accused of using a superior command of language to make Kenneth feel small. Maybe I did. Certainly, I strove to make him feel accountable, at least, to his other classmates. For all his impressive physical height, he seemed smaller in mind than the others.

I was angry because I had been forced to adopt a disciplinarian sulk and to use a scathing tone of voice that I had never had to draw on before. The truth is, I suppose, I resented the need for it and was unwilling to spoil the beneficial atmosphere of relaxed goodwill already established in that class.

Though he didn't know it at the time, Kenneth was lucky. The class he had moved into was a special, one-off group, who had all moved up from a less reputable school. They had made progress by means of hard work and determination. They wouldn't have described it so, themselves, I imagine, but theirs was a triumph of character. Not one of them could cite even a distant relation who had ever managed to sit for a 'Higher'. They aimed to be the first in their family.

Subsequently, there was some self-conscious tension, but things soon settled down. Kenneth did the work asked of him and, latterly, put in extra work for marking or discussion. He never missed a class. After a slow start, he became almost a model student. He secured his Higher. At the end of his year, he received his reward.

Outwardly, he hadn't changed much. He spoke the same, though he sounded better informed. He was popular with his peers, as he always had been, possibly - though for different reasons. He sounded more mature. Significantly, as he proved that morning, he had learned to say thank you.

He had also learned that if you want to cross from one side of the road to the other you have to face the traffic.

He learned that from his new classmates.

(A few years later, I received a request from an academic institution in Australia. I was asked to provide a reference of good character for a Mr Kenneth Scott who had applied for a post as a Lecturer. I was happy to comply)

© Copyright George Crossan 2004

Right or Wrong?   Edwin Webster

When I was a primary school pupil, teacher used to give the class a daily spelling lesson. We learned ten words a day as homework, then were tested on them the following morning. Those who got a word wrong, had to write it out ten times, until they got it right. This process turned me into a good speller; in fact, compared with 95% of today's youngsters, I think I am a master speller, a bobby-dazzler, an ace, a real crackerjack, king of the heap.

However, one day I fell foul of teacher over one particular word. Porridge. P-O-R-R-I-D-G-E. That was the way she printed it on the blackboard and that was the way I copied it into my homework book. Now, I was an observant little sod and after school that day, when I was in the corner shop buying tatties for my mother, I saw a packet of breakfast oats on a shelf and the product was called Porage. So, this word was on a label, on a packet, on a shelf, in a shop, therefore to my young mind, the spelling must be correct and an acceptable alternative to teacher's.

Next morning, she asked me to spell "porridge." I stood up confidently and spelled out "P-O-R-A-G-E." Miss X went what is now called ballistic; she went bananas, crackers, aff her heid. Her complexion changed from peely-wally to purple. She looked daggers at me. She blew a fuse. She hit the roof.

I was bemused. She tore me off a strip in front of the class; in fact, she tore several strips off me. When I tried to explain that I had seen the word spelt that way on a packet in a local shop, she called me a liar, a miserable little liar. I felt ashamed and humiliated, but I didn't cry, at least not on the outside.

Anyway, next time you're in Safeway, Somerfield, Tesco, Presto, Mace, or wherever you do your shopping, look closely at the shelves of cereal products and see if they carry oats produced by a long-established and reputable firm called Scott's. Easier still, when next you're resting your idle backside on the settee, filling your face with junk food and watching Crap-Awful TV, look out for an advert featuring a kilted Scotsman who is working in a corner shoppie. He is asked by young woman to get her a packet of Scott's from a high shelf; this necessitates his climbing a ladder, so giving the devious female the opportunity to determine whether the handsome young man is a true Scot. Check out the spelling on the packet, then tell me if I am justified in bearing a grudge almost sixty years later.

© Copyright Edwin Webster 2004

Whigmaleeries: A Word in Your Lug

The Teacher anne flann

We sat at our wooden desks, awaiting the entry of our new teacher of English. Miss Wood had left, quiet gentle woman that she was, we'd never thought of her as "the marrying kind". But we'd all enjoyed the calm, scholarly atmosphere she created, and those who wished to learn were blessed, and those few who didn't calmly wasted their time, for she never raised her voice.

The door opened briskly. "Good morning, girls." "Good morning," we murmured in response. "I think we stand up when a teacher enters," boomed the splendid voice, "or rather we will do so from now on." Thus did Mrs. Gray enter our lives.

It was never dull. And no more did those recalcitrant pupils dare to be late, or forget their homework, or drag their heels.

She was large, not fat, but built to a large-boned frame. She had elegant hands and feet, the latter in gleaming brown oxford shoes. She wore her clothes with flare. They were of excellent quality, but missed being schoolmarmish. A draped scarf of exotic shades relieved an otherwise plain sweater. Amber beads, round and smooth in rows on ample chest. Her hair was long and coiled, brown with coppery tints which glistened as she turned magnificently poised head to stare down some preoccupied pupil, who would hastily become busy. She seldom punished, it was seldom necessary for she held us in thrall. Exam standards rose remarkably and even the least competent passed.

It was her voice I remembered most. It fluctuated like a musical instrument played by a virtuoso, an expert. It rose in volume and almost boomed to drop to a mellifluous murmur the next. Whatever she read, poem or prose, Shakespeare or Dylan Thomas, it mattered not, for she had a voice for each suiting perfectly. You could not help but learn, each word like a typewriter key covering blank paper of the mind with script.

Strangely enough I was never afraid of her. Others had the ability to reduce me to nervous stammering, not so this woman who drew the best out of all, even I, timid as I then was.

Walking through autumnal countryside, my soul filled with beauty of golden sun on flaming sycamore and copper dark beech, my small daughter crunching her way through rustling leaves, I was startled by a bounding dog. A magnificent chow, black tongue lolling from panting mouth. He rushed to my child, curliqued tail wagging. A splendid figure strode into view and booming voice cried "It's all right, he's harmless, adores children." And Mrs. Gray approached like a ship in full sail. She looked not a day older but the fine brown eyes now peered myopically through thick-lensed spectacles. "Why, I remember you," the voice dropped to a pleased, warm murmur. "You're the child who used to sit, mesmerised by words, soaking up all we did like a little sponge. When you read back a passage you used almost the same inflection as I, especially poetry. I considered it a compliment." "I remember every word of Hamlet's soliloquy and Helen of Kirkconell," I replied, laughing. "They're etched forever on my mind."

We strolled a while, chatting of the past. She asked if I had gone on to university, and seemed disappointed that I had not. "You had a talent for essays, I remember. You had a gift; we should never waste any gift we're given in this life. Go home and write a story for that little charmer you have there, come visit me and bring it with you." She handed me her card and I walked away with every intention of doing as she asked.

Life has a way of throwing everything at you at once. Family illness and bereavement intervened. But I did write that story; such was the respect I held for her. Alas too late. I picked up the paper and read of her demise. I felt a deep sadness, but also a sense of resolve that I mustn't let her down. She had given me a pride in myself in that last meeting. If my writings have any merit today, it is to my old teacher that credit lies.

© Copyright Anne Flann 2004

Angus

George Crossan

Angus was worried. Or depressed? He couldn't decide. As he trudged his way to school, alone but determinedly, he knew he was deeply unhappy.

He would have given a lot to be tempted with a straightforward reason for skiving. He pushed the thought aside. Thinking of it made him feel ashamed. He had never plunked school, and he wasn't going to do it now. It wasn't Mr Burke's fault, he told himself. But it wasn't his either.

He had done nothing to create the crisis. It was an aggregation of circumstances, he might say one day, when he was older and had given more mature thought to it all. At the moment, it was an unpleasant and confusing experience. There was no self-pity, just painful bewilderment – and, perhaps, just a little inclination toward the notion that Mr Burke was exploiting this state of affairs for his own and for his fellow pupils' enjoyment.

Angus was a bright boy. That's not a phrase he would have used himself, or one he would ever have given much thought to. He wasn't a swot. Innocently, when class prizes came his way, at the end of the year, he would feel proud and pleased to have his efforts rewarded.

He wasn't aware of any competitiveness - until Mr Burke, his English teacher, started to run monthly, class exams. After a few tests, it became clear that the top first two places were shared, randomly, each month, between himself and another boy.

For reasons of his own (maybe he had his own problems), the other boy resented being second, and showed it by derisively mocking Angus, cleverly, in the classroom, in the guise of good humour. Whether it was caused by his own insecurity as a teacher, or by a mistaken desire to be one of the 'boys', Mr Burke began to inflict his own brand of sarcasm on the hapless and increasingly wretched Angus.

Angus's world began to fall to pieces around him. Mr Burke, like an animal in the chase, found him an easy target for his wounding sarcasm. As Angus lost more and more confidence, his answers became more befuddled and absurd, and he became more and more the object of class merriment. There was no one he could turn to. It was humiliating. He didn't know what to do, or how to think, about it. He was in a situation outside his experience and, apparently, outwith his capacity to deal with it; nor did he know how to share it. He was in a fog of confusion.

At playtime, he dug his hands into his pockets and plodded up and down the playground, a solitary figure, conscious of his sense of isolation from his peers, yet not able to ease the pain of it. Mr Burke is a good teacher, he would repeat to himself, over and over, ad nausium, but not able to agree within himself, that he, personally, was any worse the individual he had been before all this happened. He felt guilty but did not know what his sin was. The burden seemed irremovable.

A day came, however, when Mr Burke asked him a question, for which he had an answer. It happened a second time; and a third. Each time, he felt a little surer of himself. The fog was clearing. Another day brought a similar reassurance.

Mr Burke, maybe tiring of the chase, or finding the prey moving out of reach, eventually abandoned it. The other boys in the class, imperceptibly at first, but more noticeably later, followed his lead. Soon – surprisingly quickly - the drama was over.

Angus had bounced off a wall, and suffered pain and humiliation. But he had gained some valuable insights into the world he was to live in.

Was anyone else aware of his pain, of his acute self-doubt, of the depth of humiliation he endured, of the shock to his psyche - to his self esteem? It was a coming-out of an age of innocence. Friends can alter. Teachers can hurt. Life can be unjust and unkind.

And when no outside-help seemed available, only stubborn belief in his true identity found the answer.

Angus's view of the world would never be the same.

© Copyright George Crossan 2004

Whigmaleeries: A Word in Your Lug

R.I.P.   Edwin Webster

Many people, as they grow older, pay increasing attention to the Death Notices in local newspapers. This is due to a number of factors. Partly out of curiosity, to see if they've outlived others of their acquaintance. Partly because they know that one day their names will feature there and wondering how their own notices will be worded. Partly to re-assure themselves that they are still alive and kicking, whilst all around, others are dropping like flies, from sundry nasty and very painful conditions.

Recently I came across one particular obituary which brought me up with a start, almost a slap in the face in fact, and which evoked memories of sixty years ago; unpleasant, unhappy memories; memories of cruelty, ill-treatment and shame.

Picture a bright, sunny afternoon in June, a rural primary school, and a class of two dozen eight-year olds, twelve girls, twelve boys. The teacher, Miss F., was a harridan. In her sixties, she not only looked fierce she was fierce. With iron-grey hair, a sharp beak of a nose, and a rat-trap of a mouth, she scared every child who came in contact with her. She ruled by fear; not so much the fear of corporal punishment because she did not use the belt indiscriminately; rather fear of her caustic tongue, and the viciousness of her verbal assaults on those who tried her limited powers of patience.

On this summer's afternoon, amid the slumbering countryside, in a well-ordered classroom, a young girl asked politely if she could please go to the toilet.

"No!" bellowed Miss F. "You've hardly been inside for half-an-hour and already you want out. Didn't you go at lunchtime?"
"Yes, Miss, I did, but I need to go again."
"Well, you're not going. Not under any circumstances."
"But, Miss, please—"
"Be quiet, girl!" Thundered Miss F. "Get up and go to the front. Sit on that chair in front of the fireplace and face the class."

Downcast and shame-faced, the wretched creature rose and did as she had been ordered. After a short time, she made one last, unavailing, attempt:
"Please, Miss, I can't wait—"
"Silence, girl, and sit still. Don't dare move".

Nothing stirred. All eyes were riveted on the poor girl, isolated in her seat of shame. It was as if we were all too scared to move or breathe. Then it started. First, a few drips on the bare wooden floorboards underneath the girl's chair; next, a dribble; then a steady stream; finally a flood. Urine poured from the hapless girl, forming a considerable pool around her feet. Gradually, the stream died away until even the last drops ceased. You could have heard a pin drop. The unfortunate girl in the chair squirmed, shed noiseless tears and shook, in shame and despair. I well remember the anguish on her face.

"You dirty, filthy, disgusting creature. Go and get a bucket and cloth and clean up your disgraceful mess" howled Miss F. The pupil did as she had been told, then got down on hands and knees to mop up the liquid on the floor. She had been barely begun when Miss F's voice bawled out:

"You stupid, stupid girl. Have you no sense at all? Clean the chair first otherwise you'll get the dirt from the floor all over it. You're useless! Completely useless!"

Eventually, the ordeal was over, chair and floor cleaned, a long and frightening afternoon at an end, and the victim of a teacher's wrath was able to escape the classroom and hide her shame. However, it was never over for her. The girls in the class never referred to the incident but the boys never let her forget it. She was nicknamed "Stinky" and the name was shouted at her in the playground and the street. The worst of them invented a game whereby one of them would touch the girl in question and then wipe that hand on another boy and shout out "Stinky!" The recipient, in turn, would chase another boy and try to transfer the touch of "Stinky." It was all very silly and unnecessarily offensive.

In later years, when I encountered the woman who had once been that poor young girl, I remembered that summer's afternoon of needless cruelty. Nowadays, a teacher who acted in that way would be suspended from duty, possibly struck off the teaching register, and perhaps even taken to court.

When I read her death notice again, more carefully, I was glad to note that she had three children of her own and a number of grandchildren. I like to think that they made her very happy and that she was a fine mother and grandmother to them. It pleases me to think so.

© Copyright Edwin Webster 2004

For the Bairns...

The Whistle   Adelaide Gordon

James was having a birthday party. His mother was preparing lots of goodies for his friends. There were loads of sandwiches to make, sausages to bake, ice cream with dollops of jelly on top to be put into glass dishes in the fridge. Sweets and crisps emptied into large bowls.

James often played with his friend David and his dog Spike in the woods at the end of the road where they lived. Spike loved chasing rabbits down their burrows.

Spike was not a very obedient dog. He liked to play longer in the woods when it was time for the boys to go home. James had an idea. His grandad left him an old whistle with other little treasures. He often kept it in his pocket when he went to play.

If he gave Spike a few biscuits as a treat when he blew the whistle in the woods surely the dog would come running. The plan worked. He no longer had a problem getting Spike to come home.

James's mother ran out of bread. She asked the boys to go to the baker. They were playing upstairs on the computer. Reluctantly they set off to the shops.

After buying the bread they headed for home. Passing the woods, they heard their friends shouting and laughing.

"Let's see what they are up to." Said David.

They found some boys swinging on the long rope hanging from a stout tree branch.

The trick was, who could hold on the longest before falling into the stinging nettles below where the ground sloped into a ditch.

After chatting for a while, James reminded his pals not to be late for his party.

"Look at the time" remarked David, glancing at his watch. "Your mother will be wondering where we have got to with the bread."

They hurried along the path. James stumbled and fell as he tried to get up he yelled out in pain. "Are you okay?" asked David.

"My ankle is sore." He replied. "It really hurts." The boys went to sit on a boulder by the side of the path. His friend tried to help him to walk hopping on one foot but that did not work too well. They wondered what they were going to do. James had an idea.

By this time his parents had become concerned about the time the boys were taking to come back from the shops. His Dad went out to look for them taking Spike with him.

James took his whistle out of his pocket and started to blow it as hard as he could. He explained to David that his Dad would surely come to look for them and it was time to take his dog for his walk. If he had Spike with him, he would hear the whistle. "Good thinking" he remarked.

The sun was setting low in the winter sky, casting gloomy shadows through the trees. "It's getting a bit creepy in here" whispered David. James kept blowing the whistle. They huddled together against the chilly air.

Thinking he may have missed the boys, his father headed for home. Passing the woods, Spike became excited, wagging his tail and pulling on the leash. His father, realising the dog may have heard the boys, entered the woods.

A large shape came crashing towards the lads causing them to scream out in fright. It was Spike of course, he smothered them in sloppy licks so glad to see them.

James had suffered a sprained ankle. The party went ahead, his friends gathered round as he told the story of the little treasure his grandfather had left him. They all took turns to blow the whistle. Spike was the centre of attention, getting lots of hugs and being told what a clever boy he was. He wasn't really but he really enjoyed his extra slice of cake, which he gobbled with great relish.

© Copyright Adelaide Gordon 2004

Whigmaleeries: A Word in Your Lug

Bubba – The Lion Cub   anne flann

The tiny spotted lion cubs tumbled and rolled together, paws groping, claws sheathed; a growling, squeaking mass in mock battle in a game that teaches them survival in their jungle home.

Mother lion lay sedately nearby, watching them with a lazy, proud look while father, leader of the pride, kept a watchful eye on them, his ears twitching in the heat of the sun.

Simba and Suki were greatly respected in South Senegal where they lived in the Casamance tropical jungle area, amid panthers, hippos and hyenas. Simba is strong and brave – leader of the pride. He stands proud and allows no nonsense from his two small sons and daughter. This does not stop Bubba, the largest of the cubs, from getting into mischief. He is venturesome and sometimes naughty – one day he too will become leader of the pride. Already he bosses his smaller brother and sister, but he looks after them quite carefully too. The jungle is full of pythons, boas and hooded cobras so that other animals must be watchful while at play or in their search for food. Bimba his small brother is VERY careful to obey his mother and father and little Tinga their sister follows them in all their adventures, but is timid and often wishes Bubba didn't get up to so many pranks all the time!

They all enjoy chasing things, butterflies, birds and other small animals and they tumble and play all day till tired, when they curl up besides mother lion, cosy and safe while father guards them all. They have great adventures but don't stray far from their parents, for father would cuff them with his massive paw and forbid them a share in the day's feast he has caught for them.

One day the cubs trotted off through the long golden grasses to seek new adventures. Sun dappled the forest ferns and sparkled on the water of a stream, which rippled through the forest after the Big Rain. Bubba, of course, led the way. "Bossy Boots" Bimba called him to Tinga – but only when Bubba wasn't listening! Little Tinga found a pretty frog with jewelled eyes and poked her nose towards it, nearly falling backwards in surprise as it leapt high with a loud croak of anger. She poked it again and again it hopped nearly onto her head, so she chased and jumped after it for ages, putting on her growliest voice, pretending she was very brave – but she couldn't catch it. Bimba chewed on an old tree root which sprang back like a spring when he let go, and it smacked him on the nose. He too growled in his throat and pretended it was a deadly snake and he the winner of the battle! Finally he sniffed under the large hole in the roots and a small rodent scurried out, running round and round the trunk in its fright as Simba gave chase, but it finally popped down another hole out of reach, leaving him very cross and disappointed.

"You're SILLY," said Bubba scornfully, flexing his claws in imitation of his father and half closing his eyes to look mean. "I can catch anything 'cause I'm not a scaredy-cat frightened of a little mouse!" He flicked his long tail in disdain. He really could be rather annoying and conceited sometimes, even though his brother and sister loved him for his strength and courage, he was VERY annoying in this sort of mood.

"Oh phooey," said Bimba crossly, still smarting from the root hitting him on the nose. "You're not all that brave anyway" and he trotted off in a huff, tail held high. "Come, Tinga," he said "It's time we went back to mother – you know she told us not to go far – that python's been around a lot lately." "I'm not scared of a silly fat python," growled Bubba, angry his brother had DARED to answer him back – and he trotted off, stalking through the trees with a stiff-legged walk, just bursting for trouble and feeling as though he could tackle anything. He swiped at an enormous butterfly as he passed, not looking where he was going and WHACK, he ran right into the coiled form of the big, fat python.

Ti, the python had been lying curled, lazily watching the young cubs. If he had not just finished a large meal and was full, one of the little ones would not have escaped his hungry appetite! However he was lazy, sluggish and his narrow eyes glittered with rage and his tongue flickered from his big jaws for he was mad at being disturbed. He slithered towards Bubba who stood rooted for a moment hypnotised by the fixed stare of the huge snake. Then instinct told him to run fast and he scurried away as fast as his little legs could carry him. Pythons move fast but Ti was heavy with food so the little cub [not so brave now] scrambled up the nearest tree. He sprang from one branch to another as the python wound round and climbed the first branch. Bubba leapt and slipped, claws clinging to the branches, his heart beating fast. Beneath, the python wound round a big branch. "Not worth the effort," he hissed. "But he had better beware of me next time I'm hungry!" He coiled round the warm, mossy branch and settled down to sleep.

Bubba dropped down to a lower branch and just slid down the tree trunk. It was difficult for lions don't usually climb trees. He scurried through the trees to get back to his family, not knowing what a state his fur was in, all sticky with something gummy. Hungry after his fright and knowing he had stayed away too long he crept close to where his parents rested, but he stopped to lick his fur, for mother liked them to be clean. Oh dear, his fur was stuck in a gooey mess and he chewed and chewed, but the more he chewed, the stickier it got. It stuck to his teeth, his whiskers and his paws as he tried to tug it off. There were great lumps on his spotted tummy and even on his tail – a proper mess he was.

He chewed and chewed till he got if off, but it grew into a big lump in his cheek. "Oh DEAR," he sniffed sadly, "what a mess I'm in." As he sniffed, nearly crying, the dusty pollen from the long grass tickled his nose. "Atishoo, atishoo, ATISHOO," he sneezed and his parents and the other cubs heard him. They trotted over to see him hidden in the long grasses. They stared at him for from Bubba's mouth a large bubble grew and burst as they came near. It splattered his face and whiskers. "Atishoo, atishoo, ATISHOO," he sneezed again and another bubble blew from his mouth. The other cubs rolled in the grass, holding their fat little tummies in glee, and making squeaky laughs. Mother and father lion exchanged looks. "What on EARTH are you doing, Bubba?" Asked his mother, but the little lion couldn't speak for the wad of gum still stuck in his jaws. He chewed and chewed and at last it stopped sticking to his teeth and he spat it out.

"Well, I've never seen anything like that," Suki said to their father, Simba. She looked at her tiny cub, head hanging in shame beside her. "I think he has learned his lesson and will be a good, obedient lion from now on," she said after he told them of his awful adventure with the python," she nodded to Simba and the father lion looked VERY stern, but was trying hard not to laugh. He nodded gravely, said "All right, he can eat this time, but he must try never to be so silly again, or he will never be King of the Jungle, and I will send him away." Simba knew how lucky his son had been to get away from Ti. He stalked off to keep a watchful eye for trouble, while his family settled down to eat.

Later Tinga and Bimba teased Bubba – getting their own back for his bossiness. "Bubba, Bubba, Bubba Gum," they chanted. Do you think maybe that was how bubble gum was first discovered?

© Copyright Anne Flann 2004

Crathes Castle's Visitor   Sylvia Chesser

The spider crept across the kitchen floor. Sarah was fascinated by it, because she had just been hearing about Robert Bruce. Mrs Mackintosh her teacher had explained how Bruce saw a spider in a cave trying to spin its web. It was finding making it's web very, very difficult. However, the spider did not give up but kept trying and trying again until it succeeded. Watching the spider is said to have inspired Bruce to continue his campaign against the English. Bruce was successful in winning the next battle, which was at Bannockburn in 1314. Mrs Mackintosh said that like Bruce and the spider they should not give up when things got difficult but try, try again.

"Do you know the story about Bruce and the spider mum?" Asked Sarah.

"Yes and if you like we can go to Crathes Castle tomorrow. The land there was given to the Burnett family by Robert the Bruce." Replied her mum.

"Would they let us have a peep into the Castle? I really like castles?"

"Yes, because the castle was given by the family to the National Trust and anybody can visit there."

"When I own a castle I'll stay in it. I won't give it away."

Sarah's mum laughed and said, "We won't worry about that just yet!"

Next day, the sun was shining brightly as they drove along North Deeside Road to Crathes Castle. First they walked along one of the trails, which went along by the Coy Burn. They next visited the garden and admired all the flowers and trees. Sarah had lots of fun with some other children in the play area. She was beginning to get very excited as they were going to visit the Castle after their picnic lunch.

The guide told them lots and lots of details about the Castle including that it was a good example of a tower house. Sarah looked keenly at everything. As they wandered around the different rooms Sarah imagined that she was a Princess who lived in Crathes. In the double tower, a man asked the guide if that was the Green Room. The guide replied that it was. Sarah suddenly saw a lady with a baby cross the room. She hadn't seen her on the tour before and thought perhaps it was the guide's wife. The lady's dress was certainly much prettier than any of the other visitors. Sarah would have liked to ask the lady if she could have a look at the baby but she suddenly disappeared. The lady had a sad but friendly face. On leaving the Castle, Sarah told the guide it was now her favourite castle.

Mum said they could have a drink and a cake in the restaurant before they went home.

Whilst munching on her carrot cake, Sarah suddenly remembered the lady with the baby.

"I liked the dress the lady with the baby was wearing. When I live in a castle I am going to have a dress like that."

"Which lady was that?" asked her Mum.

"The one in the room that the guide said was called the Green Room. I remember that because the lady had on a green dress."

"I didn't notice her." Replied her Mum, trying to work out what to say. Sarah had certainly never heard of the Green Lady, so she must have seen her. Nobody else in the double tower could have seen or felt the presence of the Green Lady, as nothing was said about her and some of the people on the tour had plenty to say. Would she tell Sarah that the Green Lady was the ghost of Crathes Castle? She had heard that nobody is sure of the Lady's identity but that some people believe she was a member of the family. Some people like Sarah also see her with a baby. During restoration work the body of a woman and of a baby were found. Seemingly the Green Lady continues to haunt the castle even though her remains were freed from their place of hiding. Until today she didn't believe in ghosts!

Sarah was now saying her hero was Robert the Bruce because of the spider story and his giving of the land that Crathes Castle stands on. Perhaps the story of the Green Lady could wait for another day.

© Copyright Sylvia Chesser 2004

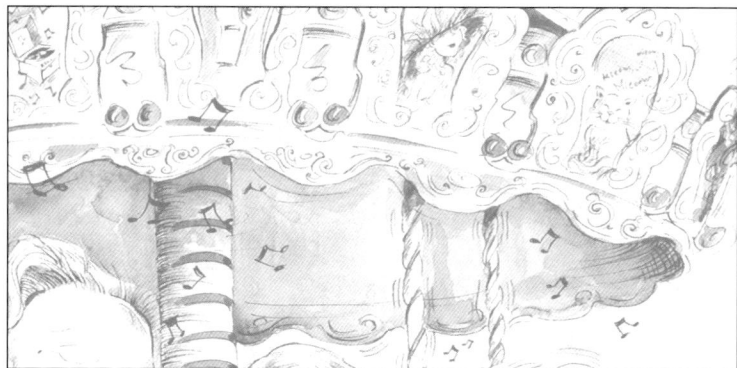

Whigmaleeries: A Word in Your Lug

The Magic Button   Clarissa Kelly

Tommy, Bob and Jodie were playing outside their block of flats in the garden. The grass had long gone leaving a covering of hard baked earth. The area was quite run down and the garden had become a rubbish tip. The people who lived there threw their discarded furniture into the garden and the friends loved to rummage about looking in the drawers to see what they could find.

On this particular day the friends were wondering what to play at when they spotted an old wardrobe which had not been in the garden the day before.

Bob ran to the wardrobe and opened the door. Inside he saw some old clothes. He pulled out an assortment of jackets and set about searching through the pockets for money. No such luck, but Tommy found a small brass button in the pocket of the long black coat he had been searching. The button had the pattern of an anchor on it and a streak of lightening. The children looked at it as Tommy held it in the palm of his hand. Maybe it's a magic button thought Tommy. He rubbed the button on the sleeve of his Gap top hoping the dirt would rub off and made a wish at the same time. "I wish we were playing in the sun." Suddenly the three friends were being whisked through space, the loud hissing of the air passing their ears making them giddy. They screamed with fright and excitement as they swirled about with their arms and legs flaying around them.

Just as the whooshing slowed down and they were regaining their breath, they landed not too gently onto a deserted sunny beach. This was great, back home they had been playing in the cold, now they were standing in the warm sunshine. As there was no sign of anyone around, the children felt free to run about the beach. They took off their socks and shoes and ran about screaming and laughing.

They decided to go for a swim as they were very hot. They took off their clothes and Tommy placed his bundle neatly folded beside a boulder on the beach. He carefully placed the magic button in the pocket of his jeans.

For the next few hours, Tommy, Bob and Jodie had great fun. They swam in the warm sea, threw stones into the water and searched in rock pools for fish. Jodie was an excellent swimmer so she swam out into the clear blue sea swimming under water among the colourful fish. Tommy and Bob continued to play in the rock pools.

Jodie came up for air and floated on her back feeling the hot sun on her body. She casually looked towards the beach for her friends. She could see them bent over examining a pool among the rocks. Suddenly her attention was diverted to a strange sight. The heat shimmer made her eyes blink, as she was not sure of what she was seeing.

Whigmaleeries: A Word in Your Lug

On the beach she could see some sort of animal. It looked prehistoric to Jodie. She shouted a warning to her two friends engrossed in the rock pool, but she was too far away for them to hear her cries. Something else must have alerted Tommy and Bob, for they jumped up and ran along the beach away from the monster. Jodie had never seen them run so fast. The monster stood on its hind legs and roared. Fire splayed out of its mouth. At ten feet high, it was huge and covered in greenish scales like a crocodile. It set off after the boys and although it was huge, it was clumsy and ambled along the sand, making slow progress.

Jodie could see that her friends had reached some caves and had entered one with a small opening to escape from the monster. The monster reached the cave but was unable to get inside the small entrance. It remained outside roaring and blowing fire and rolling its head about. It seemed to be very angry and frustrated.

Jodie swam to the shore and stealthily crawled along the sand until she came to the tree-lined edge of the beach. She was looking for Tommy's pile of clothes to retrieve the magic button. She thought it was the only way the three friends could be saved.

Where is the boulder? Thought Jodie. She was panicking now, running about searching for the clothes. The boulders all looked the same. She felt her eyes stinging and blinked away the tears, which were about to fall. She felt frustrated and frightened and worried about her friends stuck in the cave. She thought she would start systematically working along the beach rather than run about in a panic.

Jodie collected her thoughts and set about finding the elusive boulder. There it was, hardly a few feet away with the clothes folded neatly beside it. She searched Tommy's jeans' pockets and found the button. She let out a big sigh she was so relieved. "Magic button, I hope you will work for me." She rubbed the button with Tommy's top. "Magic button, get us back home please." She could hardly breathe, her throat was constricted with anticipation not knowing what would happen if the magic didn't work.

Whoosh! Whoosh! The whirling mist enveloped them all and sped them through space, landing them back in their garden. Never had the scruffy yard looked so good to the friends as they stood up and looked around them. Their eyes were bulging and their hearts racing as they looked at one another and burst out laughing. When they calmed down Tommy asked for his button. Jodie unclenched her hand expecting to see it there but her palm was empty. She searched her pockets but still didn't find it. "It looks like we will have no more adventures." Said Bob in a relieved voice. "Of course we will!" Said Tommy. "Who needs a magic button when we can create our own adventures."

© Copyright Clarissa Kelly 2004

The Charioteer   anne flann

The child was visiting her grandmother in the small compact flat near the ruined cathedral. She was petite for her age and had a great imagination. Elflike and dainty of foot she skipped through life in a veil of dreams, while her elder sisters had feet firmly planted on the ground in a world of girlish chatter, whispered secrets – and boys. Here she was alone for the first time, no parents, no sisters, and her Gran and Granpa all to herself. Grandpa was frail and scholarly, with a fund of tales to tell the wide-eyed child. History of the cathedral ruins, tales of ghosts and nymphs, of knights and maidens, and of fairy people in the nearby woodland glades.

In the high walled garden behind, a succession of children came to keep her company. They tended to boss her, a stranger in their midst. They resented being dressed up, when they'd much rather have been at the beach, or fishing for eels in the pond in the park. But they enjoyed the cup cakes baked by the granny and the home made lemonade in a large glass jug which seemed never to empty.

They played happily enough in the ivy-darkened garden, where a vine hung gazebo soon became a witch's cave, fairytale castle or Neptune's grotto, for this child never lacked ingenuity and weaved fantastic stories, acting them out – tales that would have shamed the brothers Grimm. Tired of these they would resort to climbing, running, playing hide and seek till the small girl was exhausted and ready for bed when they went their various ways.

The bedroom faced the rear of the house. The bed was high and large, seeming to envelop the girl with its massive down filled quilt. The sheets and pillows were starched, which prickled her bare arms and legs as she lay awake, past sleep. Behind the bed, a small window high on the wall gave light from the hall beyond and on the ledge of it perched the statue in bronze of a roman charioteer with winged helmet. His chariot was drawn by two rampant horses, fierce and wild-eyed. The flickering gaslights from the hall shone through this window casting shadows on the far wall of the room. The figure seemed to whip the horses to prance and rear – she could almost hear the shrill whinnies and snorts and lay transfixed, horrified but fascinated at the same time.

Sleep overcame her and she sank into that other world of dreams, vivid, frighteningly real. She heard again the neighing of the horses and heard the thud of hooves thundering near. She felt herself snatched up and into the chariot, struggling as the strong bronzed arm of the charioteer clasped her tightly, while the whip flailed the horses to greater speed. On and on they sped, she could feel the wind tear at her clothes and hair. The horses' feet were silent now, they sped up through clouded sky and beyond a glittering castle of golden towers and glistening white came into view. The clattering hooves on cobbled road told of their arrival in this strange place, which seemed devoid of people or animals. The youth led her through the streets to the gateway of the castle she had seen on the journey, gold tower beckoning from afar. Here statues of marble seemed to thaw like ice and become silent servants, bringing fruit, wine and sweetmeats which she refused to eat or drink. Her escort shook his head in despair, but tempted her with a golden goblet filled to the brim with sweet smelling fruit nectar. Thirstily she drank and the bronzed young man laughed in triumph as she swayed dizzily. He turned into a gnarled grotesque demon whose talloned fingers grasped towards her like an eagle's claws.

Terrified she turned and fled through the arched door into the street. She ran and ran as mists swirled around her and she stumbled, suddenly her feet felt emptiness and she fell, down and down through cloud and mist. Behind her she heard the angry shriek of the demon and bolts of lightening flashed from his fingers towards her. On and on she fell and screamed with fear as the thunder of hooves now bore down on her – the chariot, the horses breathing great snorts as they were whipped to greater speed. She struggled desperate through the mist, thrashing in fear – and woke to her Grandma's gentle voice soothing, murmuring "Why child, it's only a storm, don't be afraid". And was clasped in safe arms and carried away from the shadow of the charioteer, who beckoned her from the far wall.

© Copyright Anne Flann 2004

A Kitten Named George   Adelaide Gordon

It was getting dark. The cat was looking for a safe place to rest and hide. Wandering down a quiet lane she came upon a gate, which was slightly open, and she crept through. She found herself in a lovely garden where a thick bush attracted her attention. This seemed a good place to settle down for the night.

The next morning she gave birth to a lovely kitten. He was mostly white with some black marking on his back and tail. He had a tiny pink nose. His mother licked him all over, as mother cats do, and she fed him her milk. She quietly purred as her kitten snuggled close to keep warm.

Now and then she left her kitten for a short time as she knew she would get something to eat from the kind old man at the fish shop. He always left out some food for her. He felt so sorry for the stray cat that didn't have a home.

One day coming back to her kitten she wasn't careful crossing the road and was knocked down by a car.

The kitten was all alone in the bush now. He was cold and hungry and kept calling for his mother.

Katy and Cameron, who lived in the house at the top of the garden, came out to play and heard the kitten miaowing. They peeped into the bush and saw him. "Go fetch Mummy", Cameron told his sister as they both looked at the kitten.

Mummy came and reached into the bush. "Oh dear! Where did you come from? You are so tiny you poor little thing", she said as she picked up the kitten. He was frightened, cold and hungry.

They brought him into the house and fed him warm milk from a saucer.

They found a small cardboard box and a nice woollen scarf, which made a cosy bed for the kitten. He soon fell fast asleep.

The weeks passed. Katy and Cameron had great fun with their new-found friend. They named him George after a favourite uncle who used to tell them wonderful stories.

George would have many exciting adventures with the cats that lived in the neighbourhood.

© Copyright Adelaide Gordon 2004

The Three-Legged Race   Sylvia Chesser

The twins had been puzzling for days about how they could best resolve the problem of who should take part in the three-legged race. They were all going to stay for the weekend with their father's parents. The village where their grandparents stayed was having a big fun day. The villagers used to enjoy them annually but there had not been one for a long time. Everyone had been saying that the community spirit was not what it used to be and it was felt that a fun day would help. The twins, Tommy and Jimmy had been looking forward to it for weeks. There were to be races including a three-legged race for children. The twins would do the under 10 race together so there was no problem with that. In fact, they had been practising for weeks. However, they were concerned who was going to partner dad in the father and son three-legged race. Everytime they asked dad he just laughed and said not to worry about it. Jimmy thought they should both practise with Dad.

"You'll probably be better than me, you can run faster." Said Jimmy.

"That isn't fair though. You were born first." Said Tommy.

"What if we both went with Dad and had a sort of four-legged race. Doesn't matter if we don't win. It would be good for a laugh."

The twins always liked a laugh and the family had a lot of fun. They lived in a council flat and didn't have a lot of money to spare but they did all right. Their mother, Shona, worked part-time in the supermarket and their father Colin was a mechanic.

Only last week they had gone to the local shop and asked if they could do a paper round. The shopkeeper said they were a bit young yet and to come back in a couple of years time. He said the bag of papers, especially on Saturdays and Sundays with all the supplements would be too heavy for them.

"What if we do the round between us and you give us two bags? We would manage that way." Asked Tommy.

The shopkeeper laughed but said that they would have to wait a bit yet.

"We'll be back when we are fourteen. We'll manage a round each then."

Jimmy and Tommy went back to trying to decide who should partner Dad in the three-legged race. They did everything together and their parents always tried to treat them equally.

"What if Dad put our names in a hat. The first name to come out can be his partner."

"That's a good idea. We'll ask him tonight."

"Let's hurry home I'm hungry."

"Me too. Wonder what mum's brought home tonight. Hope there was something good in the Special section at the supermarket."

"Dad what about putting our names in a hat to see who will partner you in the three-legged race?"

"Don't worry. Its already been decided who my partner will be." Colin answered with a big grin on his face. Don't worry about it."

The twins thought it was odd as this wasn't like their Dad at all. He was always fair and seldom had secrets from them. He did surprise them though when he managed to fix up new bikes for them. Well not new but pretty new. He had even painted the bikes so that they looked similar and had a new sheen to them. Between their Dad's practical do-it-yourself ability and their mother's brilliant shopping the family managed okay. It did help that she knew all the best bargains at the supermarket. Not many two for one deals, or special offers passed her by.

The sun was shining brightly when the family reached the Fun Day. Colin and Shona, the twins and their grandparents had a good look around all the stalls. The children's races were first. Tommy and Jimmy managed to win the under ten three-legged race. They had practised enough and being the same height and weight helped. They watched various events before it was announced that the father and son three-legged race would be in ten minutes and for the competitors to go to the starting area.

"Which of us is it Dad?" asked Tommy

"I don't mind if its Tommy."

"I don't mind if its Jimmy."

Colin, Shona and Granny and Granda were all laughing. What a family for laughing.

"What's so funny?" asked both twins at once, "what's so funny?"

"Granda's my partner. It's a three-legged race for father and grown-up son!"

The twins joined the laughter. They hadn't thought of that one.

© Copyright Sylvia Chesser 2004

A Child's Fairy Tale

We come with the wind
To caress your hair;
And if there's a storm,
You would find us there,
Guiding the rain around your eyes,
Holding your hands
Till the sun does rise.
On its going down,
You will find us again,
Beating our wings on the window pane,
Whispering softly:
'The children sleep'

George Crossan

© Copyright George Crossan 2004

Epilogue

Finality

Finality. Finality.
I dread the crude reality
That all is finished -
ended.
My nature is offended at
Finality. Finality.

George Crossan

© Copyright George Crossan 2004

Whigmaleeries:
A Word in Your Lug

Editor: Lisa Savijn - Oral History Officer
Design: Bill Smith - Publicity and Promotions Unit
Photographs: George Crossan
With thanks to: Aberdeen Oral History Department

Lisa and the Green Room Gang.

When Les left, the void created by his departure was most capably filled by Lisa Savijn, Oral History Officer with Aberdeen City Council. Lisa coaxed, cajoled and more swiftly than any of us imagined, this slender volume took shape. We owe a debt of gratitude to Lisa, who charmed the best out of us. Here's looking at you, kid!